EXTRAORDINARY CONTACT

CONTACT

LIFE BEYOND INTRUDERS

EXTRAORDINARY CONTACT
LIFE BEYOND INTRUDERS

by

DEBRA JORDAN-KAUBLE

www.augustnightpress.com

PRAISE FOR

EXTRAORDINARY CONTACT

~

Mysterious inexplicable marks on her parents' lawn lead Debbie on a search for answers to the mystifying paranormal activity that has haunted her family for years. She reaches out to pioneer UFO abduction investigator Budd Hopkins and becomes "Kathie Davis" in his bestselling book, Intruders. Now, thirty-three years later, Debbie tells her fascinating story in her own words. A must read for anyone who has a serious interest in UFO abduction phenomena.

~ **KATHLEEN MARDEN,**
AUTHOR OF EXTRATERRESTRIAL CONTACT

Debbie takes us on a journey of self-discovery and high-strangeness, challenging us to awaken from our lives of quiet desperation. She reminds us that a mind stretched by new experiences can never go back to its old dimensions. This book is not to be ignored!

~ **REV. MICHAEL J S CARTER**, M. DIV.
AUTHOR OF ALIEN SCRIPTURES: EXTRATERRESTRIALS IN THE
HOLY BIBLE,
CONSULTANT FOR HISTORY CHANNEL'S ANCIENT ALIENS

I have known Debbie for three decades and have always been impressed by her remarkable case, and by her honesty and authenticity. Extraordinary Contact is a long overdue, up-to-date accounting of her ongoing experiences with phenomena that simply should not be, but which continue to touch the lives of millions worldwide. This compelling and timely book is a must-read!

~ CALVIN PARKER
AUTHOR OF PASCAGOULA – THE CLOSEST ENCOUNTER: MY STORY,
AND PASCAGOULA – THE STORY CONTINUES

Since my first TV documentary investigations began for the Denver CBS station in September 1979 about animal mutilations, human abductions, UFO crashes / retrievals and government cover-ups around the world, I have interviewed more than 2,000 experiencers. Those people are at first filled with shock, fear and anger about Something that intrudes, trespasses, controls and harvests them. But that Something also helps, protects and teaches. Eventually, once-terrified humans don't want the Others to leave. In this remarkable book about her *Extraordinary Contact*, Debbie Jordan-Kauble penetrates that paradox with her own revelation: "Because of Them, my mind and my soul have grown."

~ LINDA MOULTON HOWE
EMMY AWARD-WINNING
TV DOCUMENTARY PRODUCER OF *A STRANGE HARVEST*,
REPORTER AND EDITOR OF AWARD-WINNING
NEWS WEBSITE EARTHFILES.COM,
REPORTER THROUGH 14 SEASONS OF
HISTORY CHANNEL'S *ANCIENT ALIENS*.

CONTENTS

~

For Robby, Casey, Elizabeth, and Emma

ORIGINAL INTRODUCTION

Budd Hopkins

~

The month of September 1983, when I received my first letter from Debbie Jordan, seems like half a lifetime ago. So much has happened to Debbie and to me, as well as to the world's understanding of the UFO enigma as a result of those first communications. The changes have been so profound that it is almost impossible now to recall the state of our knowledge of the UFO abduction phenomena prior to the "Kathie Davis" case, to use the fictional name I gave Debbie at the time.

The 1987 publication of *Intruders* brought before the public the results of the investigation that followed my receipt of Debbie's original letter and photographs. That complex three-year inquiry produced major new information about the patterns, scope and apparent aims of the UFO abduction phenomena, data which has since been replicated in the research of independent investigators throughout the world. A brief review would include, first of all, the fact that the extensive physical evidence in this case effectively demolished the notion that UFO abductions are purely "mental" events with no outside witnesses. At the beginning of Debbie's June 1983 experience, she and her mother independently reported seeing strange lights on the Davis property. And where Debbie remembered seeing the landed UFO, the ground was affected in peculiar ways: the grass died, and, below, many cubic feet of moist, dark soil was changed into grayish, rocklike material that for years was unable to support vegetation. Extending outward from the roughly eight-foot circle of alters soil—the spot where the craft apparently rested—was a forty-nine-foot straight swatch of similarly damaged earth. This evidence dramatically supports the idea that the object Debbie saw that night left behind clear-cut physical traces and was, therefore, neither a fantasy nor a dream.

To support that notion, when the craft apparently lifted off, Debbie's next door neighbor saw a brilliant flash of light through the trees at the location of these ground traces. Seconds later, as some kind of craft passed noisily overhead, the neighbor's home suffered a complete power outage. Equally strange, all the lights spontaneously came back on, with no disturbance to either fuses or circuit breakers. This neighbor's testimony further eliminates any suspicion that the event can be regarded purely as an artifact of Debbie's mental processes.

In the days following her abduction, Debbie experienced a series of unpleasant physical aftereffects suggestive of low-level radiation poisoning. But it was not just Debbie who experienced such problems— the behavior of birds and animals around the affected soil was unusual, to say the least, and the lesions and severe hair loss that her dog suffered led to its eventual death. Debbie tells the story of these physical sequelae at some length in the following pages, as she, her sister, and her family experienced.

Even more important than the fact that this case demonstrates the physical reality of UFO abductions is the evidence pointing to a long-term alien reproductive experiment. Prior to 1983, a few investigators were aware of a sexual or reproductive component in some of the small number of abduction reports that had been investigated: I had run into such suggestions as far back as 1976. Yet, most abductees had been reluctant to volunteer information about this highly personal aspect of their experience. And, since investigators hesitated to bring up the subject, issues of reproduction and sexuality had remained for years in the margins of our knowledge of the abduction phenomena. In a pioneering decision, Debbie Jordan was the first woman to fully reveal this most intimate aspect of her ordeal. Her uncommon courage has made it easier for hundreds of men and women since then to unburden themselves, thereby immeasurably aiding UFO research and facilitating the work of therapist and investigators.

What Debbie's account revealed is no more or no less the central reason for alien interaction with humans. Despite alien curiosity about human sexuality, our own basic maternal and paternal instincts, and about the way human beings form relationships with one another, it is our genetic makeup that appears to be the focus of alien attention.

The story of this watershed event has been told fully in Intruders, so there is no need to present it here. What has never been made public, however, is the background of Debbie's decision to allow this part of her story to be included in my book. The details of her disappearing pregnancy and the later presentation to her, inside a UFO, of what she took to be the hybrid result of that pregnancy comprise the most personal and poignant saga one can imagine. Nothing Debbie said during the many months of my investigation was as moving to me as her description of what it was like to have her baby forcefully taken from her, and, years later to feel the sudden rush of maternal love for the strange but beautiful little girl the aliens presented to her... and then the profound anguish of separation as the child was once again taken from her.

One night, as the investigation was winding down, and I began to discuss my ideas for a book about her case, Debbie seemed thoughtful and quiet. After a long pause, she said that there was one thing she did not want me to write about. She asked me not to include anything about the little girl, whom she had named Emily, and about whom her feelings were still too raw, too sadly troubling. Her love for this child and her sense of helplessness at having been separated from her were still too overwhelming to handle. She wanted none of this—the pregnancy which vanished and her short, precious meeting with Emily—to be included in a book that strangers would read and skeptics would deride or even ridicule. It was a private tragedy that she was not yet able to share.

Believing as I did that information about alien genetic experimentation was the single most important issue for our knowledge of the phenomenon, I asked her if she would agree to a tentative compromise. I promised to continue working on the book with this part of the story included, but added that after I'd finished the manuscript, she could read it and if she still wanted me to, I would delete the sections dealing with her missing pregnancy and her involvement with the little girl.

With this understanding, I continued writing, hoping that she would change her mind. And then one night, as we drove together to an airport, Debbie was unusually silent. I don't remember her precise words once she began to speak, but they were something like this: "Budd, I've been thinking a lot about Emily and my pregnancy and that whole thing and I've decided that you can put it in the book. I know this has happened to a lot of other women, and I sure know they must feel like I do. It's about the saddest and strangest thing you can imagine. In one way I don't want this part of me and my life to be so public, but this is the way I've come to think about it: Maybe I'll never do anything great in life, or have a chance to have an effect on things in any major way. Maybe this is the one really important contribution I'll ever be able to make... to let other people know what happened to me so they can understand what might be happening to them..."

As we drove along that night, Debbie spoke very softly, as if there were literally months of thought behind her words. I knew how moved she was, and how much her decision cost her. There were tears in my eyes too.

In the years since then, Debbie has become a role model for hundreds of other abductees, frightened, confused men and women who have seen in her a strong, very human and vulnerable young woman who has survived and ultimately triumphed. If she can face these devastating problems and surmount them, so can they. The trajectory of her life follows an ideal line: From the low point of stasis and depression and denial, she lifted herself up and ahead to face her disturbing memories and fears. In 1983, she wrote her letters, throwing several away until she was able, finally, to mail one. And then, feeling a little safer, she began to explore her experiences. She met other abductees, formed new friendships, but faced new bouts of denial and depression all interspersed with a steady sense of gain over the confusion she'd lived with for so long.

Understanding her feelings more clearly and moving away from the helplessness she's known for so many years, she agreed to let her story be known for the good of untold numbers of other men and women. It took a while longer for Debbie to gather the courage to speak in public for the first time about her experiences. But that seemed to her to be a necessary next step in facing—and facing down—the fears that had nearly crippled her for so long.

I remember vividly that first public appearance, in 1988, at one of John White's conferences in North Haven, Connecticut. Debbie had asked me to stand at the podium next to her for moral support, and when she stepped up to speak there was a period of silence. "I've never done this before," she told the audience, "and I'm really kind of scared. Just let me take a minute to get myself together, and then I'll be all right." I'm not sure if these were her exact words, but that was the sense of what she said. She lowered her eyes and was silent. We waited. The silence deepened. All the people in the audience were leaning forward, tense, inwardly wishing her well. The silence continued, and then she looked up, smiled, and said, "I'm okay now," and began her relaxed and wholly natural talk. At the end, there was a standing ovation. Everyone sensed that hers was an unmistakable voice, a voice of honesty and humility, a voice of simple wisdom. It is the voice that one finds in the pages of her book—a work that represents the current stage in the lifting trajectory of Debbie's life. The confidence she has acquired over the years is fully revealed in the limpid directness of her forceful writing.

The appearance of her sister, Kathy, as a co-author is yet another demonstration of the strength and resilience that UFO abductees so frequently possess. In Kathy's case—as in Debbie's—it was not always so obvious. When I first met Kathy, she was both wary of my investigation and curious to find out the meaning of so many odd fears and memories that had inevitably colored her life. After some tentative interviews and regressive hypnosis, experiences that she movingly describes in the pages of this book, Kathy decided against a more extended exploration. It was clear she felt that the privacy and well-being of her husband and children might be at some risk if she allowed an investigation. However, it also seemed to me that she was fearful of what might be discovered if she allowed the process to go forward.

In clear, eloquent prose Kathy lets us see into her mind, helping us to understand why she ended the investigation a decade ago, and why, now, she feels strong enough to tell the full story behind her decisions. In a certain sense Debbie and Kathy represent two diametrically opposed responses to the same stimulus: the first, the path of openness and risk; the second, the path of caution and privacy. And yet now, a decade later, the sisters who chose opposite paths find themselves in exactly the same place, sharing with the world their years of private anguish and their present sense of slowly building strength.

Over the years, I've learned many things from my investigations into the UFO abduction phenomenon. I know that some kind of nonhuman intelligence is interacting with us, but on its own terms, telling us only what it wishes to, and manipulating us with cold objectivity. I also know that some part of our government is aware of these intrusions and depredations but for its own reason is deliberately denying this fact to the public at large. There is a sad and depressing parallel here: the government lies and the aliens lie. Each, apparently, has a hidden agenda: neither can be trusted.

But if the issues of government secrecy and alien intentions occupy the thoughts of many investigators, I find myself thinking far more often about the victims of both, about the pain they've suffered and the strengths they've shown. I think of Debbie and Kathy, two sisters from a modest Midwestern family who suffered greatly but who finally triumphed—two marvellous representatives of the bravery and resilience of the human spirit. I am proud to have known them both.

—Budd Hopkins
New York, 1994

FOREWORD

Yvonne Smith

~

When Debbie asked me to write the Foreword for her book, I was very touched and truly honored. I feel that I have known Deb my whole life.

Many years ago, when I read her book, *Abducted! The Story of the Intruders Continues*, I was awestruck learning about what happened to her and her family from her personal point of view. You'll hear her return to "June 30, 1983" throughout this book like a refrain. It was the day her life changed. She sees a strange light emanating from the pool pump house in the backyard. She decides to investigate to see if anyone is there and finds no one. Then a sudden feeling of panic sets in, she turns to leave to get back to the house... but freezes. What follows is a chain reaction of missing time, haunting visions, bizarre visitations, and surreal manifestations that go beyond the typical profile of a "close encounter," and bring into question everything we seem to know about it.

My work as a hypnotherapist is concerned more intimately with the human element of these experiences. Like so many people unaware that they have been abducted, Deb began having nightmares and seeing images of big black eyes. Every time she looked at the strange, lingering mark in her parents' backyard, it triggered these confusing and frightening memories. Once you begin to pull the thread, there's no going back.

Alien abduction is an intergenerational experience, something as inexplicable as it is perturbing, as Deb talks about in her book. Paternal and maternal grandparents, mothers and fathers on both sides, their children and their children's children. This experience affects millions of people all over the world with startling similarities regardless of the language they speak.

The more I worked with abduction cases, the more I recognized Deb's physical and emotional reactions as typical of someone experiencing Post Traumatic Stress Disorder (PTSD) due to a traumatic event. As a hypnotherapist, I have worked with clients who have suffered from physical abuse, sexual abuse, horrific car accidents, and military returning home from deployment. They seek help because they experience flashbacks that they do not understand, and nightmares or reoccurring dreams which often lead to insomnia, irritability, and extreme anxiety. The symptoms of PTSD are all the same. Alien abduction is no different.

While the physical reality of abduction itself is enough of an ordeal to process, Deb also talks about her lifelong paranormal experiences that occur in tandem. This aspect of the abduction phenomena may surprise many people, as many deem it necessary to isolate one phenomenon from another, but this connection is nothing new, going way back with researchers like the late John Keel and D. Scott Rogo. In the thirty years of hosting the CERO Support Group meetings, members had countless discussions about hearing cabinets in their kitchen opening and closing, toilets flushing on their own, hearing footsteps when no one is there, disembodied voices, and so on; typically deemed poltergeist activity. I myself even started to experience it in my home when I was married, and my boys were in elementary school. Whether this was a result of having these meetings in my home, and, hosting these individuals under the same roof while they spoke openly about their experiences, I can't say.

During one CERO meeting, a couple of members told me that they had dreams of "crashing sounds" and "glass breaking." Now I must stress here that when abductees report having similar or even the same dream, it's usually a strong indication that something has happened or that something will happen. That night, in the wee hours of the morning, my family were jarred out of their beds by a loud crashing sound. It woke us all out of a dead sleep. We went running toward the dining room to see what happened. As we looked down from the top landing of the stairs, we saw that the large mirror above the fireplace had somehow separated from the wall and came crashing down on the floor!

Like Deb, and perhaps unknown to her up to this moment, one of my sons also witnessed a "spider" in his room, which also scared him enough to sleep in my room on a regular basis.

I have learned over my thirty years of working with abduction cases, that paranormal and UFO experiences go hand in hand, and all too often it gets pushed to the side as being too far out there, even for people interested in UFOs. But it begs the questions: which came first, and what's the connection? I just know that when I'm working with abductees and they tell me about the strange goings-on in and around their house, I reassure them that I am not surprised; this is par for the course, and they certainly are not alone.

These are the things abductees need to hear. Without that confirmation and reassurance, their lives quickly spiral out of control as they fail to grasp what's happening to them. Their nightmares begin to invade their everyday lives, refusing to be ignored, turning into waking memories, screaming out from the subconscious. They often have no support system and nowhere to turn.

Where would Deb be today if it weren't for Budd Hopkins? I shudder to think. I pride myself on being a beacon for those like her, as Budd had been. He taught me how to give them the tools to cope and heal without invalidating or minimizing the extraordinary reality of their experiences.

Like Deb so eloquently shares, I too feel that my connection with Budd was guided by destiny.

In 1988, my mother, Rose, asked me to accompany her to the Whole Life Expo in Los Angeles. These were paranormal/metaphysical conferences held around the country. My mother wanted to attend this particular one because it was being held at the Pasadena Convention Center, very close to where we lived. Marquee names included Timothy Leary, Uri Geller, Terence McKenna, and Louise Hay. My mother, though, wanted to see the UFO speaker named Budd Hopkins. I had never heard the name, but my mother, steeped in metaphysics, UFOs, and the paranormal, knew exactly who he was, and she was looking forward to his lecture. I agreed to go and like the old saying goes...the rest is history.

I was dumbfounded by the information he was presenting. As the New Age community basked in the warm and fuzzy glow of the recent

Harmonic Convergence, Budd was laying down a strange and harrowing reality: one that included drawings by people who claimed to have been abducted by aliens. After his lecture, I introduced myself to Budd and I will never forget how he graciously took the time to answer my questions as he was surrounded by people who were anxious to speak to him. He was very patient and kind.

In 1991, I received my certification in hypnotherapy. I had the good fortune to have Budd as my mentor, often inviting me to observe his regression sessions; valuable training I did not learn at the hypnotherapy institute, to say the least. As I began working with clients who had vague and unsettling half memories, I felt a tremendous responsibility toward these stable, highly functioning individuals who were desperately seeking answers.

All through the 1990s, I was asked to speak at various UFO conferences, which included Budd Hopkins, David Jacobs, and John Mack. As the "rookie" of the group, I cannot stress enough how invaluable it was to sit with these heavy hitters in the field and compare notes and ask questions for clarification about abduction cases to ensure that I was on the right track.

Back before I read Deb's book, I too was one of the tens of thousands of people who became enthralled with Budd Hopkins book, *Intruders: The Incredible Visitations at Copley Woods*. And for those of you who remember, in 1992, it was made into a CBS miniseries—a two-night event.

Budd would often come to Southern California as a guest speaker and would sometimes stay in my home with my husband and my two young sons. It was during one of these visits that Budd asked if I would join him and director Dan Curtis in a lunch meeting to discuss the *Intruders* miniseries. The main actress, Mare Winningham, who played Mary Wilkes (Deb's character), called and asked if she could observe one of my regression sessions. She was concerned about how she should react as a person "reliving" the abduction experience.

In the early years of my practice, I conducted the regressions in my home. Mare came over and met my client who agreed to have her present during a live regression. Not too long after this, I was invited to visit the set of *Intruders*. I watched as Mary Wilkes (Mare Winningham) was taken onto the ship where she was introduced to her little hybrid daughter. Watching this scene, I had tears in my eyes the moment Mary realized that the little girl being presented to her was her very own. I recounted all the times I sat through gut-wrenching sessions with clients who were introduced to their hybrid children and the realization that their child could never live with them on earth.

Not too long after *Intruders* premiered on television, I met the real Mary Wilkes who was, of course, Deb Kauble. I felt as if I already knew her from my many conversations with Budd while he was visiting, from reading his book, *Intruders*, and from being on the set of the miniseries. I don't think Deb knows even to this day how I admired her bravery, coming out of the shadows to share her story with the world.

In 2013, CERO International was launched, the public branch of CERO Support Group. We hosted lecture events for the purpose of educating the general public about abduction. Even with more mainstream acceptance regarding the UFO topic than ever before, abductee accounts are still shunned and ridiculed, or altogether ignored; relegated as a fringe topic within a fringe topic.

In October of 2016, we invited Deb to California to be a speaker for our "Faces of Abductees/Experiencers" event. Because I was receiving inquiries, I asked Deb to ship some of her books so she could have a book signing after her lecture. When she told me that she didn't have any copies and the publisher had gone out of business, I told Deb that she *had* to revise and update her book. She has such an important case, and the public is anxious to hear from her!

As you read through *Extraordinary Contact: Life Beyond Intruders*, you will be captured by her deep emotions and confessional storytelling. Deb takes you through her personal Pandora's Box, from the very day her life changed up to the present day, as she continues to share her ongoing experiences, and how they've defined her.

From my work with Budd, and through the hundreds of cases over the past three decades, what is clear is that the UFO phenomenon runs a tremendous 180-degree gamut: from being totally physical (landing traces, markings on the body, photographs, radar signatures) to totally paranormal (telepathic communication, craft and beings that dematerialize, abductees floating through walls, missing time). It is this apparent contradiction that we as researchers have the hardest time reconciling. But we must shed light on the seemingly impossible.

As Budd once said, "The whole paradigm of what's possible has to be expanded." I believe that expansion lies in the personal and subjective experiences of abductees like Deb. It is time to empower such individuals who have the courage to disclose what's happened to them throughout their lives, and to use these experiences as a platform to explore the phenomenon further. This will lead not only to revelations about who these visitors are, but, more profoundly, who we are—as a species and as spiritual beings.

Budd Hopkins did not provide us with answers but showed us the path. The work and resilience of Debbie Jordan-Kauble honors that guidance and trudges forth through the mystery that lies ahead.

—Yvonne Smith, C.Ht.
Author, Lecturer

PREFACE

~

The original version of this book, *Abducted! The Story of the Intruders Continues*, was published in 1994, and it included several chapters that were written by my older sister, Kathy Mitchell. You will not find those chapters in this book. The original manuscript, which I wrote by myself, was already finished by the time Kathy had expressed an interest in including some of her experiences. I tried to encourage her to write her own book at the time, as I didn't see any way to manageably incorporate her words into mine without starting the book from scratch. But Kathy insisted, so, being the loyal little sister that I was, I agreed.

Kathy has since suffered from some very serious health issues that have pretty much ended her writing career. Indeed, sadly, Kathy's condition is such that she can no longer even care for herself. This has been the biggest factor in my decision not to include her chapters in this updated book. If she had any other experiences beyond those she shared in the original edition, none of us knows about them, and she is no longer able to tell us.

As soon as I decided how I was going to approach this project, it quickly gelled together in my mind and I realized that this would actually be more of a rewrite than a revision—more like a brand-new book. Herein, you will find all of my original work, documenting my own personal perspective on the event of June 30, 1983, the event that led Budd Hopkins to write his bestselling book, *Intruders: The Incredible*

Visitations at Copley Woods (1987), which later would be adapted as CBS miniseries (1992).

But you will also find a lot more here. My story didn't end in 1994 when the original edition of this book was published. In the three decades between then and now, my extraordinary contact has continued, and it has spilled over into the worlds of the paranormal, premonitions, near-death experiences, synchronicities, and government surveillance, not to mention everything that life in general has thrown at me over the years, from marriage and divorce, to suicide and tornadoes. Here you'll read about how extreme emotional and even physical trauma have been woven through the tapestry of my life and served as fuel for my personal growth and transformation.

It is my hope that, by sharing in my journey here, you'll see that *you can* overcome anything that life throws at you. You can emerge from the shock, fear, and chaos of your experiences in one piece—calmer, wiser, and more in tune with yourself and with the world around you.

—Debra Jordan-Kauble,
January, 2021

ONE

The Mark

~

Fourth of July weekend, 1983. This was the start of the odyssey that would become my life. As I looked at that huge mark in my parents' back yard, a million thoughts raced through my mind. Somehow, I knew what it meant, I knew how it had gotten there, yet still I couldn't believe what I was feeling—panic and confusion—and what I was *seeing*... Big. Black. Eyes.

"That's where our UFO landed," said Mom.

Hearing those words from her, spoken so casually, I slammed back into reality, my heart skipping a beat. My father was bitching about how his beautiful yard was ruined now, wondering aloud if he had somehow mowed the grass too short. Typical dad. He had this obsession with his lawns. Ever since we'd moved into this house he had pampered and protected his beloved grass as if it were his favorite child. I swear, sometimes, at night, I could hear him talking to the seed, nurturing it. God help those responsible for this travesty.

Meanwhile, I was beginning to recall how the yard had gotten so messed up, and I didn't like what I was remembering. These emerging memories were too much like the nightmares I'd been having lately... and that was just unthinkable.

The whole family had come over for a celebration picnic. Later, we were going to set off fireworks. This had become something of a family tradition since we had moved in. Our house was the only one big enough to accommodate the whole family. It also helped that we were in an area where the houses were spread far enough apart so as not to set the neighborhood ablaze with our spectacular display of K-mart

1

explosives. This was the first time anyone had been in the backyard since the night of June 30—the night I saw the light in the yard. The night I believe the mark in the grass to have been made.

June 30

Four Days Prior

That night—June 30—I had been getting ready to go to my friend's house to do some sewing. I was divorced and living with my two sons at my parents' home. My friend had launched a lucrative little costume sewing business and I was her assistant. At that time in my life, this was my only source of income, meager as it was.

I was standing at the kitchen window, washing chicken grease off my hands, when something caught my eye, outside in the backyard. I noticed a strange light emanating from the swimming pool pump house. Now, the light in and of itself might not have been so strange. But because I had been out there earlier that day, loading the pool with chlorine, and because I distinctly remembered wrestling with the rusty slide-lock on the pump house door, I *knew* that the door shouldn't have been open. Later, I was to learn that the light bulb fixture in the pump house didn't even work and had been burned out for several years.

I called to my mother for her to look at this strange light in the pump house. She joined me at the window and noted that indeed it *was* strange, although she didn't seem to too concerned by what she was seeing. It was a very bright, white light that seemed to have a life of its own. It appeared to radiate through the open door, in bursts.

I had a strange feeling that I had better stay home that evening, but I shook it off and left anyway to visit my friend. As I got in my car, I decided to drive back behind our house on the turnaround, just to make sure that I didn't see any prowlers lurking about. As I made my turn and approached the back of the house, I saw that the light was gone, and, to my surprise, the back door to the attached garage was now open. I don't know why I didn't stop right then, but I didn't. I drove over to my friend's house, approximately two minutes away from our home on the street directly behind mine.

As soon as I arrived at her house, I called my mother. I told her what I had seen and asked her if she wanted me to come back. I was thinking about burglars. Mom insisted that everything was all right—that she would lock the doors and keep the porch light on for me. She told me not to worry. I hung up the phone thinking that all was well and started to tell my friend what I had seen. No sooner had I hung up when the phone rang again. I grabbed it on instinct. It was my mother; she sounded scared. She asked me to come home, "right now." This was not at all like my mother, someone who was scared of nothing. As I talked with my mom, my friend's husband could hear my concern, and he yelled from the bedroom, "Why don't you call the police? That's what they get paid for." Hearing this over the phone, my mother told me, "I don't want anyone here, except you."[1]

I jumped in my car and raced home. The trip took all of two minutes. When I got there, I pulled up alongside the house and jumped out of my car, right at the back-patio door. Mom was standing there, waiting for me. I went into the patio, grabbed my father's shotgun, and started back through the kitchen to the porch. Mom told me that the gun wasn't loaded.

"Well, I'll just beat them to death, if I have to, I replied." For me to have even gone out there that night was strange—totally out of character for me. I am the biggest chicken who ever drew breath, and normally I would have run the other way. Plus, I hate guns with a passion and always used to complain to my father for even having them in the house. For me to actually grab one with the intention of using it, in any way, was not like me *at all*.

I proceeded to go from the back door of the kitchen over to the pump house, out by the pool. I don't remember seeing anything strange in the yard at that time. I forced open the rusty lock and stuck the gun through

---

[1] What my mother had failed to tell me during that phone call, but which she would recall almost a week later, was that, after I had left for my friend's house that night, my mom had watched the strange light in the pump house *go out*. Soon thereafter, there appeared a soft, basketball-sized white light that surrounded the bird-feeder directly in front of the kitchen window. My mom had tried to figure out the source of the light—perhaps it came from a car or a flashlight, but she soon realized that there was no beam. The glow seemed self-contained. Self-luminescent. As she stood there watching this light, it grew fainter and fainter, until finally it disappeared. It was only then that she got the idea to call me home from my friend's house. Several days later, she said to me, out of the blue, "Oh, by the way, Debbie, I just remembered why I called you home the other night." After hearing her full story, I said, "Gee, thanks, Mom. If I had known that, I would have NEVER come home, again!"

the tiny opening I had made. I yelled out some pretty raunchy threats and then kicked the door open with my left foot. There was nothing in there that I could see in the dim light of the moon. As I turned to look at the open pedestrian door of the attached garage, I realized that my dog, Penny, should have been in there. But, with the door open, surely she was out now. We'd been keeping her in the garage at night as she was in heat—we didn't want to have to get rid of yet another litter of unwanted pups. She was the Irma la Douce of the neighborhood.

I decided to look for Penny in the back lot of our property. It was a little strange that she hadn't already found me. Usually, when I go outside and she's out, she's on me like stink on garbage. I was her "Mommy." I was the one who fed her. I heard some whimpering coming from under Dad's old truck. It was parked in front of the workshop, in the back lot. I looked under the truck and there was Penny. I called to her several times, but she absolutely would not come out from under the truck. That was really strange. I grabbed her by the legs to pull her out and she fought me like a mad dog. Finally, I gave up trying. I was starting to have a real uneasy feeling about this whole thing; it was beginning to feel like another bad dream. I decided to go back toward the house and check out the attached garage. Someone could have been hiding in there. I made the same kind of approach to the garage that I had made to the pool pump house. I spewed a few obscene remarks and flung open the door as I hit the light switch. Nothing. Not a soul to be seen. I walked around for a minute or so, looking behind boxes and old mattresses. Suddenly, I began to feel very hot. It felt as if the skin on my body was burning off. I felt real panic race through me like a shot in the arm and I thought to myself, "Damn, I gotta get outta here, *now!*" As I turned to run out the door, I froze. My next conscious memory after that was walking up the back steps and thinking about my kids. Were they all right? I saw my mother standing in the open screen door, and I remembered telling her, "It's cool."

"Good," she said, "now I can go back to sleep."

Suddenly, I no longer felt like sewing. For some unknown reason, I wanted to get wet. I felt grubby and hot, so I decided to have my friend come back to my house to swim with me. I went back to her house to fetch her and, within twenty minutes, we were on our way back to my place for a dip in the pool. No mention was made of the amount of time I had been gone. It was only later that we all began to realize that I had been gone much longer than I had remembered. A trip that should have taken all of fifteen minutes had taken longer than an hour.

When we got back to my house we headed for the pool, immediately. As we walked across the yard, my friend's daughter jumped suddenly and yelled, "*Ouch!*" She had stepped on something that seemed to burn her foot. She said that it felt prickly and that her foot then started feeling a little numb. We were in the pool for around ten-to-fifteen minutes when, suddenly, we began to feel sick to our stomachs. Just before this, I had noticed that my eyes were starting to burn and my vision was "turning white." All the lights that I looked at had a halo effect around them and it felt as if I had glass in my eyes. Not unlike the effects that too much chlorine water would have on your eyes, except that I hadn't gotten water in mine, and this was much more intense. We all felt creepy. My friend even remarked that she felt like someone was watching us, so we finally gave up and ended our swimming for the night.

The next morning, I awoke with the ugliest eyes you have ever seen. They were swollen shut and running like a faucet. The pain was so bad that my mother took me to the emergency room of the local hospital. The doctor immediately sent me to the eye specialist, who saw me within ten minutes. As he examined my eyes, I could see the look of bewilderment and concern on his face. He asked me, twice, if I had looked into the arc of a welder. When he asked the question a third time I snapped back at him that of course I knew better than to ever do something so stupid. My eyes had apparently been burned, so far as the doctor could tell. He prescribed several medications and gave me instructions on how to care for my eyes. It took several weeks for them to heal and I had to make a return trip for a follow-up exam. My eyes have never been right since. They remain very light sensitive and weak. I have problems with night vision and sometimes I find that my eyes water, ache, and burn for seemingly no reason at all.

~

That was the strange night that I kept thinking about as I looked at the mark in the yard a few days later, on Independence Day. I found myself thinking about my sister, Kathy, and what she had seen in 1965, and how we razzed her half to death over it. I thought about the book that had scared me so much—the one I had tried to read several weeks earlier.

I had made a habit of going to the library a lot over that past year. It was inexpensive entertainment and we lived right across the street from one of the better libraries in the city. My children liked for me to take them there once or twice a week for story-time. While there,

I would browse the shelves for anything that might capture my interest. One book in particular had caught my eye. It had a bright orange cover with big, bold title lettering: "MISSING TIME." I also glanced at the word "abduction" on the cover. I assumed it was some kind of crime mystery.

I have a rather unusual way of choosing books. I read the last page first before looking for any drawings or photos that might be included. Then, I just scan through the rest of it, randomly, until I pick up on something that grabs my attention.

Toward the back of *Missing Time*, my eyes came to rest on a notation; it stated that if you felt you'd had an experience similar to those featured within, you could write the author, Budd Hopkins, and he would try to get back to you.

How odd, I thought. Why would anyone who had been abducted want to tell *this* guy? Wouldn't they just call the *police*? I didn't realize what kind of abduction Hopkins was talking about. When I flicked through the picture section of the book, my skin began to crawl. My first instinct was to put it back on the bookshelf, and that's exactly what I did. Throughout the afternoon, however, I felt drawn back to that shelf. So, before I checked out of the library for the day, I grabbed the book and put it in my pile of selected titles.

Later that evening, after I put my kids to bed for the night, I again opened the book and began to examine the pictures more closely. Something about them was so hauntingly familiar. Creatures with big, black eyes. Every time I looked at them, I started to panic. I tried to read a few lines but I had to stop. Each time I tried, I'd start to hyperventilate and get dizzy. This went on for several days before finally I gave up and put the book down for good (or so I thought). It turned out that *Missing Time* was about people who had been abducted by *aliens. In UFOs*. "Right. UFOs," I thought, incredulously. And yet, why did that book scare me so much? And why had my mother mentioned UFOs in reference to that strange mark in our yard?

~

As I looked at that mark in our yard on Independence Day, I began to have one of my nightmares, right there and then. All I could see, superimposed on the mark, were two huge, black, almond-shaped eyes. So lifelike, so real. It was as if they were trying to tell me something. I was trying to make myself remember, and it was making me sick.

I wasn't feeling very well, physically, anyway, and I sure didn't need *this* too. My stomach was queasy a lot, and I'd had diarrhoea something fierce. My head hurt and I hadn't been able to sleep or eat much. My whole body ached. I felt like I was losing my mind. I'd already been under enough stress as it was. I'd gotten divorced the year prior and moved myself and my two little boys back to my parents' home. I was trying to figure out what I was going to do with my life and doing my best to make two families get along in the same house. It was taking a toll on all of us.

I had signed up for group therapy at the local hospital to learn how to cope with my anxiety and all the changes we'd been through. I was hoping to gain enough self-confidence to land a good job and raise my kids, alone. In retrospect, I feel sorry for those people who were in my group. In 1983 I was wrestling with something a lot bigger than just a divorce. Now, I realize why I've suffered for so long with anxiety and low self-esteem. I was exhibiting symptoms of post-traumatic stress disorder (PTSD), even back then.

One evening, while in my group meeting, around June 30, 1983, we were listening to some poor fellow talking about how upset he was that his wife had left him. He didn't think he would be able to live without her. It really pissed me off! I remember thinking, "You wimp! You don't know what it's like to be scared. You have no idea! You think you can't make it without her? You're scared to be alone? Well, let me tell you something, buddy, you don't know what it's like to feel fear until you've felt the kind of fear I live with every day." Exhibiting incredible insensitivity, I jumped up and screamed just that, right in his face, and then ran out of the room like a wild woman. I plopped myself down on the front porch of the house where we were holding our meetings and bawled my eyes out.

I felt like such a fool. I didn't mean to hurt that guy's feelings or diminish what he was going through. I just couldn't hold it in any longer. My counselor came out onto the porch and put his arm around me as I sat there, sobbing. I'll never forget the look on everyone's face as I ranted and raved. I was so embarrassed. He told me that he wanted to help me, but that I had to remember what it was that was bothering me so much, and that I had to tell him. I couldn't remember anything that I had the nerve to tell him, and so I could tell him nothing. I asked him what it felt like to go crazy.

I'd like to make an important point. Once I began to work with Budd and all the other fine researchers and doctors, I began to learn how to cope with my feelings, and I got better. That's more than I can say for anything I or anyone else has ever tried. I think that says a lot for what Budd was doing, how he did it, and what he discovered during his investigations. Whatever he did, it worked, and I'm a lot different now. Back then, though, my kids were driving my parents crazy, and my parents and my life were driving *me* crazy. This mark in the yard was beginning to feel like the straw that would break the camel's back, and I didn't even understand why. That just made it worse, because I hate not being able to understand something.

I decided that there had to be a reasonable explanation for what had happened in our yard. I dug out the trusty old Yellow Pages and began calling anyone I could think of who might help explain it all away. I called the agricultural agent for the state of Indiana but was told that he was out of the office for a while. I called several local universities and asked to speak to their agricultural departments. I explained to them that this mark had appeared in our yard, just out of the blue. I told them that it was an eight-foot diameter circle with a forty-eight-foot long by two-foot-wide swath coming off the east edge of the circle. The swath extended south from the circle and ended in a perfectly rounded tip. The edges were very well defined and it had not changed shape since it appeared. The grass inside this mark was folded down on itself as if it had been crushed. And the soil had a particularly pungent, bitter odor. I also explained that the grass outside the mark appeared normal except for a small area directly west of the mark. This area was near the attached garage and looked as if it had been dusted with something that just scorched the tips of the grass, but which didn't burn it up or crush it, like in the mark itself. I also told them about a section of trees directly north of the circle that had been damaged. In a swath of trees about ten feet wide, the leaves had begun to turn yellow and wilt from the trunk to the top. Of course, I left out the weird nightmares, seeing the light in the pump house and getting sick. I didn't tell them about how my friend's daughter's foot had burned as she walked over the swath that night and how she began to get nauseated and feel her lower leg go numb. I knew in my mind that this was all connected and that somehow UFOs had something to do with it. But, I realized that I would never be able to convince them of that; and besides, I wanted a real answer, not something cooked up to pacify a crazy woman.

The answers that I received from various agents from different schools was practically the same. They explained to me that it couldn't have been a mold spore or any kind of fungus because they generally just don't appear all at once, and they will grow and change shape to some extent. Also, they all agreed that they had never heard of anything affecting the soil like ours was affected. The dirt wouldn't even hold water. It just rolled off it like it would a rock, and the soil was like that to a depth of some twelve inches. They had no explanations whatsoever. Everyone could tell me what it wasn't, but no one would even offer a speculation as to what it *was*, and no one was willing to ever come out and test it.

I called the local power company, the local gas company, and a few local lawn care services. I even checked with the weather service to see if there had been any lightning anywhere in our area that night that might have hit the ground and made that spot on our yard. I also asked them if lightning would do that kind of thing to a yard. I think they thought I was nuts.

I must have inherited my propensity for trying to make things "fit" from my dad. He, too, was running his own kind of investigation on the appearance of the mark in his yard. He discovered that the drainage tiles underneath the mark had been broken, smashed in many places. Shortly after the night of June 30, 1983, the transformer atop the utility pole next to the mark in the yard blew up. When the power and light company came out to repair the damage, they were mystified to see that all the wires running to the transformer had been melted together. The man my father spoke to could not explain how this could have happened. He was as perplexed as my father, who had been an electrician for 35 years. My dad was also an amateur radio operator, and he noticed that the antenna switch in the house had been destroyed, presumably by whatever had destroyed the wires outside.

Several days had passed, and every time I looked at that mark in the yard I could feel myself getting increasingly anxious. I had all but given up on trying to find an explanation for it. My thoughts continued to drift back to the book that I had looked at a month or so before the mark had appeared, before the night of June 30 when I had the strange encounter with the lights in the yard. The book that had scared me so much: *Missing Time*.

Recalling the address in the back of the book, I decided to write to the author, Budd Hopkins. I had begun to feel that maybe there was something going on in our family that might be of interest to him. My nightmares had begun to seep into my waking state and I had begun to have what I considered to be flashbacks. I could be involved in the most mundane task with my mind blank and suddenly start to see vivid scenes whiz before my eyes as if I were watching them on a movie screen, with me as the unwilling star. Sometimes, I would see only eyes—these huge, liquid-black eyes, boring a hole straight through me. At other times I would see whole faces, these grey faces with slits for mouths. I began to remember seeing bright, flashing lights, and hands, strange hands moving across me. I could almost see, again, these faces, intimately close to my own, "talking" to me in some unknown manner. I could see balls of light moving all around me and dark shadows moving about my parents' yard. I had memories of being hit by "lightning," right in the chest, and thinking that I was dying. Imagine, trying to do the dishes while you're being hit by lightning! I could actually feel the pain, over and over. Each time I'd relive this, I'd *really* relive it—feeling, hearing, touching, the whole nine yards. I'm sure that anyone who had been watching me when this would happen would have assumed I was completely nuts. I began to feel like there was something right on the surface of my subconscious that I couldn't remember, but that if I didn't, I'd burst. It was like trying to remember the name of a song that's on the tip of your tongue, but you just can't get it. Every time you think you've got it, it's gone. And you can't stop thinking about it.

I went back to the library and got that book. I raced home with it, promptly found the address in the back and wrote it onto an envelope. Then, I began to write a letter—a letter that would change my life forever. Had I known what I was starting when I wrote that letter, I'm not sure I would have. At that point in my life I was nowhere near ready to go through what I went through during the investigation. Although, I must say that now, I'm really glad I did it.

I had no idea what I was expecting Budd Hopkins to do for me. I can't figure out if I wanted him to confirm my suspicions about the night in the yard and the mark that it left behind, or if I wanted him to tell me that it was all just a bad dream that would go away and that I wasn't crazy, after all. Perhaps, I just wanted to know that I really wasn't as alone as I felt I was in all of this.

I was not experienced at writing letters of that type, just as I am not experienced as an author, so, needless to say, several letters were written which found their way to the trash can. I figured out a way to write it without personally shouldering all of the craziness that I was trying to relate to this man. I focused a lot on my sister's experience in 1965 when she had been taking Mom to a bingo game and had seen a UFO on her way home. I couldn't actually say that I had seen one myself, because I couldn't remember all that happened to me that night. So,

I decided to tell him about her at the beginning, thinking that maybe he wouldn't throw the letter away if I could tell him about her actually seeing a UFO first. Then, I'd spring the weirder stuff on him later in the letter. I was also thinking about how my sister was going to kill me if she ever found out that I had told a complete stranger about that night in 1965. She was real touchy about this particular event. We teased her a lot about it for years.

When I had finally finished a letter that I considered readable and acceptable, and after I had received the fifteen photographs I'd shot of the mark back from the drugstore, I asked Mom to mail the package. She told me later that she'd had no intention of mailing it, but when she went to the mailbox to send off some checks, she remembered that she had the letter in her purse and just dropped it in. She doesn't know why she did it after she had already decided that she wasn't going to. I'm glad she did.

From the time the letter got mailed, to the time I actually heard from Budd, I continued to grow steadily worse. Physically, I found myself nauseated every day. I broke out in mysterious rashes and began to notice that my hair was breaking off and falling out at the roots at an alarming rate. I dreaded washing my hair every morning because I couldn't believe how many times I would have to clear the drain of my hair so the water could empty out. It was getting more difficult to do anything with at all, and I was getting to the point where I didn't even care what it looked like. I had begun to sleep a lot during the day and stay up all night because I felt safer sleeping during the day, when other people were up. I would check on my kids several times during the night, sometimes sitting by their bed for hours, watching them.

At this point, I still didn't know what it was I was so afraid of, but I knew that I could never let my guard down or *they* would be back for me or my kids. I began to notice that I felt very uncomfortable whenever I got near a dark window, especially the upstairs bathroom window that overlooked the mark in the yard. I refused to swim in the pool after dark and that was something I had loved to do before the night that light came. I had also begun to go out in the evenings when I just couldn't take it anymore. I guess I just needed to get away from that house and those unconscious memories that were eating me up inside. I didn't go out as much as I would have liked to, since the kids were so little, but I went whenever possible. I had one girl friend I would go out with. As it turned out, she was also one of the people that I had an encounter with back in 1977, before I married my first husband (more on that later).

A lot of times I wished I could go out, but I just didn't feel well enough to get dressed, let alone *dressed up*. Three times in one week I went to the local emergency room thinking I was having a heart attack. I wasn't, of course, but I was having massive anxiety attacks. It's pretty bad when the local hospital employees start to call you by your first name when you walk through the door. I started having irregular heartbeats; they became so bad that one night I wound up in CICU. That condition was diagnosed as "nervous heart syndrome." I was put on a couple of different beta-blockers and the condition is now under control. Basically, I was a mess.

I was never so surprised in my life as when my mother told me, "the guy who wrote that book" had called. I hadn't expected to hear from him at all! At the very most, I expected some kind of note thanking me for my letter, but that he just didn't have time to look into it right now. But, a *call*? *Wow*!

Did I really want to talk to him? Would he think that I was just another nut? What in the hell would I say? Maybe I'd find out he was the one who was nuts, and then where would I turn?

Budd was very polite on the phone. I could tell by the way he talked to me that he was trying to get me to tell him more about myself and the night that prompted me to write him. I kept trying to change the subject back to my sister's experience in 1965. I think I must have answered more questions from him that night than I've ever been asked in my whole life! He was definitely very thorough.

Soon after I had talked to Budd for the first time, I called my sister. I told her that I had heard from the guy who wrote the book and I confessed to her that I had told him about her sighting in 1965. I figured she would be mad at me, and, boy, was she ever! But I knew that he would want to talk to her about it, so I told her to expect a call from him. It was too late to take back what I had written to him. Now it was time for me to face the music with her. "Oh well," I thought. "She'll get over it." Typical sister response.

~

My life was crazy before June 30, 1983. After that, it *really* went off the chain. I know there are plenty of other folks in the world whose lives have been much harder than mine, and I am grateful for what I have. But my life has *sure* not been boring, and not always in a good way (as you'll learn in the following chapters). The upside is that I've had a lot of life experiences, from which I've learned a great deal. I sometimes wonder if my UFO and paranormal experiences have enhanced my ability to cope with the rest of the crap that life has thrown at me over the years.

I have, from time to time, sought help in coping with my anxiety and with the PTSD with which I was eventually diagnosed. Many times, early on, I would address the obvious issues at hand, but I would not talk about the *rest* of my life, the *weird* stuff. I guess I thought it was better than nothing at all. At least I was given the tools to help cope with the general anxiety. I figured panic and anxiety were feelings, not events. And while there was more than one event, at least I could use these tools for the stuff I still couldn't make myself talk about. It sounds silly now, but it *did* work for a long time. In some weird way, I think going through the traumatic UFO events made the more "normal" traumas a little easier to bear. After all, once you've stared into the face of something so absolutely terrifying, so strange and unbelievable— something that simply *doesn't exist* in our consensus reality—then something as recognizable as a tornado doesn't seem *that* bad, right?

The June 30, 1983 event was probably my most spectacular event. It had the most physical evidence, it was the most traumatic, it inflicted the most severe physical and psychological damage, and it had (eventually) the most witnesses. That was the one event that served as a springboard for pushing me out into the public eye. It was the event that shook me awake. As the years have passed, my experiences have been taken to a different level. The actual physical contact that was happening in the 1980s and 1990s has morphed into something that feels more cerebral, even more spiritual.

I believe that some of the earlier experiences might have done some actual physical damage, specifically to my eyes, although I do not think the damage was by any means intentional—more a side-effect of the method of contact. I was subsequently diagnosed with cataracts *and* (dry) Macular Degeneration. This was by the time I was 35. By the time I was 50, my vision was so bad that it required lens replacement in both eyes. There have also been a couple times in my life when I thought that maybe the experiences had actually done some good for me. You'll read a little about that in later chapters.

I do still suffer from anxiety in relation to health issues. I remember how quickly my dog deteriorated after that night, and I can't forget how bad my eyes became. I was diagnosed with Multifocal Fibromuscular Dysplasia of the right renal artery, also at about age 50. FMD, as it is more commonly referred to, is a rare vascular disorder. Patients with FMD have abnormal cellular growth in the medium and large arteries of the body. It can cause arteries with the abnormal growth to look like a string of beads. The arteries become narrow and interfere with blood flow. The beads (aneurysms) can rupture and the condition can become life threatening. My condition was treated by balloon angioplasty and now I am monitored yearly and will be for the rest of my life. *No one else in my family, on either side, has this.* I'm certainly not saying the experiences caused this condition, but in the back of my mind, I wonder *"why me?"* I guess that's probably normal, under the circumstances.

Make no mistake about it, some of my early experiences, and particularly that of June 30, 1983, were terrifying, to say the least. I had no idea what was going on, why it was happening to me, and if whatever it was would *kill* me, at that moment, or later in my life. It left me with physical and psychological issues that I *still* deal with today, nearly 40 years later. Still, I have to acknowledge the positive changes that came from learning how to navigate this unknown territory, to find my way, and myself, in the process.

When I have spoken in public, I am often asked, if I could choose *not* to have had these experiences, would I? The answer is, I wouldn't change a thing. *All* of the experiences in my life—UFO, paranormal, as well as the other major events I have been through over six decades—have shaped the person I am today. I am awake, aware and connected in a way that I could never have been if I had *not* had these experiences to propel me. And I am deeply grateful for this. I am still a work in progress, and I'll be so until the day I pass on to the next adventure. But, certainly, I have come a long way in 62 years.

You can't always choose what happens to you, but you *can* choose how you will respond to it, and *that* is where your power lies. And it's why I wanted to update and expand my book. I have come so far and grown so much since I wrote the first edition. I feel that if I can help just one person to find some good in whatever is scaring the complete shit out them, help them to realize their own potential, then I'm doing what I'm meant to do.

TWO

Budd

~

My heart pounded as I dialled Budd's phone number. When he answered, I nearly hung up on him. Nervously, I introduced myself and explained that I had written to him, that he had phoned when I was out and that I was returning his call. I hoped he would carry the conversation from there. That phone call seemed to go on forever. I kept trying to place the focus on the photos, on the mark in the yard and my sister's encounter in 1965. He kept trying to get me to talk about *me*. I felt like a jerk.

That call turned out to be the first in a long line of calls that would take place over the next few months. In order to save money on phone bills, I began to write to Budd as well. He set me up with a "buddy," someone I could call and talk to about what had happened and how I was feeling. I really liked "Mary" (a pseudonym). We seemed to click, right off. Mary had been instructed not to tell me too much about what she had gone through, so as not to "contaminate" my subconscious. Despite this, we never seemed short of things to talk about.

As the weeks passed, I began to recall things that had happened when I was a child; things that, at the time, seemed normal to me but in retrospect were, indeed, strange. I couldn't believe how I had forgotten these little incidents. I remembered how, when I was a child of four or five, I had been frightened by a dream I had in which I thought a giant pterodactyl flew over my house and was looking for me. I remembered a trip I had taken with my older sister when I was six or thereabouts and how I had gotten lost. While I was trying to find my way back to where I should have been, I ran into a strange house and met a little boy with

15

big, black eyes who tricked me into what I thought was a playroom. He performed experiments on me and hurt my leg by poking something into it. I remembered waking up one night and seeing someone big standing next to my brother's bed, staring very intently at him, then closing my eyes quickly and feeling him do the same thing to me; his face, right next to mine. I was petrified! I remembered waking up in my bed one night when I was really young and seeing someone lying beside me, trying to suck the breath out of me through my mouth. Whatever or whoever it was they weren't much bigger than me but they had a funny shaped body and large head. I couldn't believe I had forgotten all these strange memories! And somehow, they seemed to make much more sense now.

One night I was in my room upstairs, watching TV. I heard something—a vague, beeping noise in my head, and then I heard my name being called by several voices, in unison. They were neither male nor female. They pierced through all my mundane thoughts, from out of nowhere. It was all too familiar and it scared the hell out of me. I bolted up from my bed and rushed into the bathroom. I sat in there for a moment and tried to regain my composure. "Go back to bed and relax. You're imagining things," I told myself.

As I was going back to my room, across the hall from the bathroom, a small ball of bright, white light whizzed past my head. It had come from my son's closed bedroom door and went towards the stairway. It disappeared as it began to go down the stairs. I jumped, bolted to my mother and father's room, opened the door and told my mother (who was trying to sleep) that my chest was starting to hurt again. (I didn't want to tell her about the voice that I heard. I was still trying to deny that I'd heard it because it just sounded too crazy). I asked her if she had seen the ball of light and she remarked, "It must have been lightning. Go take an aspirin and go back to bed. You'll be OK."

I knew it wasn't lightning because there were no windows in the hallway, and, besides, the weather had been nice all day. I decided that to keep waking them up would be useless and inconsiderate, so I went downstairs to take an aspirin. While I was walking through the living room to get to the kitchen, I noticed a bright, white light, right outside the living room window and I thought I could see a silhouette of a small man standing in the light. I grabbed the phone and proceeded to call my buddy, Mary. God bless her heart. It must have been one in the morning and she was as sweet as she could be. I was hysterical. She talked to me for a good forty-five minutes. Every once in a while, she'd ask me, "How are you feeling? Can you still see the light? Do you hear anything? Do you have any Valium or some wine?"

I don't know how I made it through that night, but with Mary's help, I did. We talked until I couldn't talk any more. We talked about anything and everything under the sun, anything to get my mind off what I was feeling. I don't know if anything happened after we hung up, but I slept through it, whatever it was and that was okay with me.

Eventually, Budd decided that I needed to go to New York, where he lived, so that I could be hypnotized by a psychiatrist who he knew was willing to help me, free of charge. I prayed that she would tell me I was crazy. At least *that* could be treated. Budd was beginning to realize that my June 30 incident, and my sister seeing the UFO in 1965, were only the tip of the iceberg—fleeting, tell-tale signs of something much bigger and more incredible than anyone would have ever imagined. I was so desperate for help that I agreed to go.

Of course, it was my responsibility to pay my own way there, and I was almost broke. I decided I would sell my washer and dryer to raise money for the bus ticket and food. They were the only things I had in this whole world worth more than two cents. (I must have had a guardian angel watching over my finances, because I had exactly 34 cents left in my pocket when the bus pulled into the station back home in Indianapolis. I cut that one *real* close).

~

In October of 1983, I left for New York City. I was scared half to death. This was the first trip I had ever taken solo, and I was terrified of getting lost and stranded in a strange place (something I still worry about today). Hell, I almost had a panic attack in the car on the way to the bus station! I just didn't know if I really wanted to go through with this. I was afraid of what I'd find out, and I was concerned about how I might handle it. I was worried about leaving my kids. Without me there to watch over them, what would happen to them? What would happen to me if "they" found out what I was doing? What would happen to me and my family if anyone else found out about this? Surely, we'd be the laughing stock of Indiana? This guy I was going to see, was he okay, or was he even crazier than me? He could have been some kind of psycho, for all I knew. I was taking some big risks in going to see this guy, but I had to believe that everything would be okay. I was so desperate that I was willing to risk it all, in the hope of finding a way to live with the situation—or to be rid of it—once and for all. I had to, for myself and for my kids.

New York was one hell of an experience all by itself. I had been born and raised in Indiana, but had never been any farther east than Ohio. From the moment I saw the huge skyline of New York City loom over the horizon, I was in culture shock. The bus trip itself took every bit of seventeen hours, and after the first couple I was ready to get off almost anywhere. For one brief moment, as the city towered upon me, I seriously considered turning around and going home, right then and there. I was overwhelmed, to say the least.

When I stepped off the bus, Budd was there to greet me. I recognized him right away from the picture in his book. I was very relieved to see a familiar face in the crowd, but I couldn't help thinking, "What the hell am I doing here? This is crazy. I must be crazy!"

Newspaper under one arm, his hands cradling stiff coffee and muffins, Budd guided me through the bus station and onto the subway that led back to his apartment. My first subway ride was a "trip" all of its own. I was so jumpy from the long bus-ride and all that was on my mind; I nearly went through the roof of the subway car when the lights went out for the first time. Nobody told me this was normal. Budd must have been at least a little amused at my reaction. I think it also helped him to see just what kind of state I was in at that time.

Budd and his family were very kind to me throughout my whole stay with them. I don't know of any other researcher who gives nearly as much of themselves to their subjects as Budd gave to me during the investigation of our case. I feel very lucky to have found him.

As soon as I dropped my bags in my room, it was time to go to the doctor's office. Not a moment was wasted during the whole time I was in New York. After all, I only had one washer and dryer. Who knew when I would be able to do this again?

∼

My first hypnosis session was extremely nerve-wracking. I was exhausted from the long, bumpy bus trip and I was afraid of what might come out under regression. Also, my sister had a nasty experience with hypnosis several years earlier while trying to lose some weight. I was afraid that I, too, would have a bad experience, and I sure wasn't ready for that right then. Especially not so far from home!

Not a whole lot came out during this first session, but it was enough to give me a taste of what hypnosis was all about. When we were through for the day, I felt more comfortable about it and, after a long nap, I was ready for more.

As it turned out, much was accomplished during this trip and the many that followed. Consciously, I recalled the night in April of 1978 when I had seen two grey, big-eyed creatures in my bedroom, standing next to my bed. I had told my husband about them the next morning and he asked me what I had eaten before bed that night. He didn't remember a thing, even though he had been lying in bed right next to me during the whole experience. Strangely, I never once had the presence of mind to wake him. I believe it was then that we realized I had only consciously remembered the tail end of a much more detailed event. To this day, I don't remember most of it. While under hypnosis, I had recalled feeling a sharp pain in my head, right behind my nose. I remembered tasting blood in my mouth and feeling as if something was going up one of my nostrils. I felt very cold, and I had to use the bathroom. I also saw those eyes, again—those huge, black, shimmering eyes that I could never forget. The men in my room that night, in April '78, they had those same eyes.

While in New York, I also got a chance to meet my "buddy," Mary, face-to-face. The first thing I did was to apologize for the late-night phone calls, and I was glad to see her smiling at me when we shook hands. She invited me over to her apartment for dinner one night and I experienced a breakthrough in my memory while I was cutting up salad veggies. I suddenly began to remember all kinds of little details that had been locked away in my subconscious for many, many years. I got increasingly anxious as I related to Mary all the things that I was recalling. She, in turn, was also getting pretty anxious, also. She was glad that I was remembering things that, evidently, I needed to remember. At the same time, I got the feeling that I was flipping her out a little with my spontaneous recall. Still, she hung in there with me and I'll never forget her for that. I can never thank her enough. I think it was that night with Mary that finally convinced me that my family and I were actually having real encounters with something truly anomalous. It was fascinating to see how everything was beginning to fall into place, beginning to make some kind of sense. I had come from a family historically steeped in strange happenings, and I had assumed that *everyone* lived like this. Boy, was I in for a rude awakening!

When Budd deposited me on the bus home, he left me with the comment that, "once we start to look into your case, the 'visits' will stop." I knew this was meant to make me feel better, but, honestly, I actually felt worse leaving New York than I did when I arrived. I now felt as if I was a very bad girl—that I had told something I shouldn't have, to someone I shouldn't have, and that I was going to be in *big* trouble when I got home. I felt that "they" were going to come back for me and they were going to be *mad*. I wasn't even supposed to remember this stuff, let alone tell anyone about it, especially someone who might stop it from happening again.

~

Budd passed away on August 21, 2011. The day I got the call was one of the worst days of my life. He had played such an important role in who I had become that losing him almost felt like losing a parent. We weren't *that* far apart in age, but the way he took me under his wing, gave so much of himself in his research of my case, and cared so genuinely about my wellbeing and my family, it was hard to *not* think of him as a part of it.

Near the end of his life we didn't speak to each other as regularly as I would have liked. He was unbelievably busy with his research, writing more books, travelling to conferences and attempting to pursue his art career in a more stable place. I sometimes felt as if I didn't want to worry him with little things. Because I knew he *would* worry. He had *so* many people desperate for his help at that point that I felt I could be more useful by following his lead and paying forward all the wonderful, compassionate support I had received from him.

He called me personally when he first got the diagnosis of kidney cancer. He wanted me to hear it from him before I read about it on the Internet. He wanted to reassure me that the cancer was contained, that his kidney would be removed, and that he would be just fine. Spoken like a true protective father figure. It was sweet of him to think of me and care about *my* feelings when he was going through so much himself.

He got through his surgery and life went on. Then, I got another call. He wanted to tell me that he had been diagnosed with lymphoma and that he was on the fence about taking treatments for it. I think I recall him telling me that his doctor had assured him that it was a very slow-progressing cancer. Budd felt that, at his age, he might be lucky to have just as many years with the condition or without it, but that his time

20

might be more comfortable without the treatments, which may have made him feel *worse* than what was then currently ailing him. I told him I understood, but I couldn't wait to hang up the phone because I didn't want him to know that I was on the verge of tears.

Years passed, and we were fortunate enough to see each other several more times, at various conferences around the country. Although, he was in such high demand at these things it really was hard to steal a few private moments to catch up. But we managed. And I tried to make sure I called him from time to time, just to check in.

Then, out of the blue one day, I received a package in the mail. When I saw it was from Budd, I couldn't wait to get it open. It was a copy of his new and final book, *Art, Life and UFOs: A Memoir.* When I opened the book, a letter fell out. It was several pages long and hand-written. It was from Budd. In the letter, he told me that he felt he didn't have much time left in this world and he wanted to tell me how he felt about dying, how he felt about me and all that we had been through together. And he wanted to personally say goodbye. The letter was priceless and touching and I *still* get a lump in my throat when I read it. When I had first met him, when I was so in awe of his art, he had made me a collage of my very own Guardian. I will treasure that letter, and that collage, until I die. I am so grateful that both survived the tornado.

I wrote a tribute to Budd, which I posted publicly on my website in 2011.

> Budd Hopkins has passed away. This is the message I got at 5am this morning. At first, I thought I was just not fully awake and had misread it. No, I was not mistaken. That is what it actually said. I knew this day would come. I knew he was very ill and had been for quite some time. And I know that he has been blessed to have lived a long, full 80 years. But still, all that just never really makes it *not* hurt any less. I could tell you about how he single-handedly changed the face of UFOlogy with his cutting-edge research. I could tell you how his work set the bar for all those who have come after him. I could tell you how brave he was to have put forth his ideas and theories about UFOs and the possibility of alien contact, *way* before it was acceptable...
>
> But now I need to get personal for a minute. I hope you'll understand. I'm sitting here, alone in my office, fighting back the tears, feeling like I just lost my dad again... when I have an epiphany. I would not be sitting here if it weren't for this man. I would have never met my late

husband without Budd's intervention in my life. K.O. first learned about me through Budd's book, *Intruders*. After reading it, he decided he just *had* to meet me.

I wouldn't have moved to Kokomo. I wouldn't have the great job I have now at GM. I wouldn't have gotten involved in MUFON or MRIPA, or ever have met just about everyone in my life now that I love so dearly. I wouldn't have met the man I am married to now because I wouldn't have been here. I wouldn't have written my own book about the experiences I have had, or even believed I could. I wouldn't have traveled the world. Hell, I might not have even survived this life had it not been for Budd. I was so overwhelmed by anxiety when I found him that I was barely able to function. Because he came into my life fairly early on in his career as a researcher, I was fortunate enough to have been able to get a lot more of his time and attention than those who came after me. Budd was one of the most compassionate, generous, loving people I have ever known. He took me under his wing, brought me into his life, sometimes, I think, to the chagrin of his then wife, April. And yet, eventually, she too even accepted me as almost one of the family. They invited my own little family up to the cape one year. My two little boys were forever changed by that absolutely wonderful experience. What a gift the Hopkins family gave us that summer.

Right after I graduated from Cosmetology school I took another bus to New York to see Budd and talk more about the experiences I had been having. He and April made me a special celebration dinner to commemorate my graduating and taking the next step in my life to a single, independent mother. He made lobster and we had wine! I had never eaten lobster in my life and had no idea how to even approach it. And I had never tasted such a fancy wine! Acting as the father figure he was, he proceeded to crack open the shells for me and showed me how to eat the meat with those tiny forks. I got kind of queasy hearing the shell crack and I remember seeing him studying my face intently and getting a little bit of a chuckle out of watching me experience this for the first time. See, that's the thing most people don't realize. He didn't just help me cope with the strange experiences I had endured over the years of my then short life. He exposed me to the world in ways that I would have *never* been privy to without him. He took me to big, fancy NYC art openings. He taught me how to eat lobster. He held my hand as I rode the subway for the very first time. He introduced me to culture and people that I would have never gotten to see or meet had it not been for him. He taught me to be confident in myself, to hold my head high and believe in myself. He took me with him all over the country and more. Before I met him, I had only been to Florida and Kentucky. Whether he knew it or not, he had not only given me back control over my life, but he had a huge hand in molding the person who was going to live it.

I distinctly remember one trip to NYC to visit with him and talk about possibly writing a book about my experiences and those of my family. I recall the two of us sitting on the floor of the studio where he did his art. He had been showing me some of the stuff he had been working on. I was just amazed at his immense talent as an artist, and he had given me a small cardboard collage of one of his larger pieces, to take home as a gift from him. He looked at me for a moment and then told me he had something he wanted me to see. He left the room for a moment and came back with a medium sized cardboard box just jam packed full of letters. He dumped the letters out on the floor in front of me and then told me these were some of the responses he had gotten from the book, *Missing Time*. I asked him if my letter had been in that box and he said yes, it had. I asked him why me? Out of all these people, did he choose to answer *my* letter?

"That, kid," he said, "is the 64,000-dollar question."
"Fate?" I said.

"Maybe so... maybe so," was his response. We just sat there looking at the letters and at each other for the longest time. I think we both knew, at that point, that we had some kind of a shared destiny in all of this. Budd spent more time at my parents' home in Indianapolis than I did in NYC during the three years he researched for *Intruders*. He was a master storyteller. He could mesmerize an entire room when he spoke. My parents were particularly fond of him and very much enjoyed his visits. Many a night was spent around the kitchen table, an endless pot of coffee brewing and standing room only as Budd told of his experience as a witness and as a researcher, *and* as an artist living in NYC and the Cape (my mother spent a lot of time on the east coast as a child and could relate to many of his stories. Incidentally, they were just a few days shy of being the same age). He was also a superb listener. When you spoke, he locked eyes with you and the compassion just poured from him. I always thought it must have been so hard for him to listen to so many traumatic stories and not let them get to him, as he was so empathic.

As the years passed, our times together became fewer and farther between. He had a hundred different people pulling him in a thousand directions. At first, I felt like a lost pup, but I quickly realized that there were a whole lot more people out there like me that needed him and I started using the tools for coping that he had taught me, and was soon on my way to helping others in my shoes.

As I got older, I sometimes didn't always agree with every theory Budd had or every stance he chose to take, but I never stopped loving him or ever lost sight of just how important he was, and always would be, to me. So much of who I am today is because he chose to give of himself, his life, his time, even his own money. Thank you, Budd. I will always hold the memories of you close to my heart. I will always be grateful to you for everything I have and everything I am. I will always remember you. And, hopefully, I can pay forward some of what you so generously gave to me. Go rest now. You've earned it.

DEB JORDAN-KAUBLE
AUGUST 22, 2011

THREE

The Journey Begins

~

As the bus pulled out of the station that night, I cried like a baby. I felt about as dark and dreary as the rain pouring down my dirty bus window. At least, in New York, I had felt safe. I figured, in the big city, with so many people around, "they" would never find me, and I'd be safe. Now, I was headed back to "the boonies," where I'd be a sitting duck.

I found out that Budd wasn't a psycho maniac, after all, but I hadn't decided if I believed all that I had remembered while I was there. It all sounded too crazy to me, and yet, at the same time, it all made sense. I was more confused now than before I left home.

The first stop was somewhere in Pennsylvania. As the bus pulled into the station, I thought, "I'll be damned if I'm going to share my seat with one more smelly, toothless Neanderthal!" I pretended I was asleep and I flopped my big old self all over that seat. "Let's see someone try to move this!" I was in no mood to be nice to anyone and I didn't want to have to talk to anyone, either. I was all talked out.

Everyone who was to get off at this stop, got off, and, within minutes, I could hear—and feel—new passengers boarding. I lay as still as I could and even tried to muster a few fake snores, for effect. Suddenly, I felt very strange. This prickly sense of anticipation washed over me and I got the distinct feeling someone was boarding the bus who I needed to see. I peeked up over the back of the seat in front of me and what I saw nearly took my breath away. There stood the most beautiful man I have ever seen. And he was looking directly at me as he walked up the steps of the bus! It was as if he knew I was there before he even got on the bus.

He was about 6'4", medium build, yet slim. He had shoulder-length, wavy, medium blonde hair, steel blue eyes, and the most perfectly structured face I have ever seen. The way he smiled at me really knocked me out. I thought to myself, "Well, by God, if I have to share my seat with anyone on this bus, baby, I sure hope it's you!" Then, I realized that I was staring at him, so I immediately ducked back down behind the seat. Once again, I felt like such a jerk.

Within a minute or so, I felt someone looking at me; you know what I mean? I looked up and there he stood, right over me, with that big, ornery grin of his! My heart just stopped. I immediately scooted myself over on the seat, hoping that he would sit down next to me. But, instead, some soldier, back from overseas, jumped in from nowhere and sat next to me. With a mouthful of food, half of which he spat all over me as he talked, he said hello and began to tell me all about his latest tour of duty. I looked at the stranger and thought to myself, "Oh, great!" I was thoroughly disgusted now. Then, I noticed that the stranger had sat down with my seat-mate's buddy. I could hear him talking to the buddy, and I couldn't believe what I was hearing. He said, "I see that you are very tired after your long trip. There is an empty seat right over there. If you like, I will trade seats with your buddy and you can take that empty seat. That way, you and your buddy can get some sleep. I don't mind sitting with the young lady."

Everyone agreed to the swap, and soon I found myself sitting next to *him*! He promptly turned to me and said, "Hi! I felt sorry for those guys. I knew they were tired. But I really wanted to sit with you. That's why I got them to trade seats." There was that smile, again! I couldn't take much more. With that, he asked me what I had been doing on my trip, and where I had been. I didn't want to tell him about UFO stuff, so I just told him that I had been in New York, visiting friends and doing a little snooping around. He promptly threw his head back and laughingly said, "Oh, the extraterrestrials will love that!" I dropped my jaw (I'm sure that was attractive!). I looked at him and said, "Excuse me! I never said anything about extraterrestrials. Why did you say that?" He just looked at me again with that smile. "Never mind," he said.

This was only the beginning. I was about to embark on the wildest trip of my life, and "Lars" would be the most unusual person I would ever meet. Unfortunately, I have to use a pseudonym for this strange, wonderful man I met on my journey home. I never did seek permission to use his real name (if indeed it was his real name).

As the bus pulled out of the station, Lars began to ask me all kinds of questions. He wanted to know what I did back home, if I was married and if I had any children. I managed to get in a few questions myself, before I completely slipped under his "spell." I found out that he was 33 years old, that he liked to ride motorcycles on ice and that he worked for a friend who owned a motorcycle courier business in Cincinnati. He told me that he loved children and that he thought it really must be neat to have a little piece of you live on after you're gone, in a child. He said that he had been somewhere on the East Coast, visiting a friend whose child had been involved in an accident and had sustained some brain damage. He claimed he knew of a clinic there that had been doing research on the brain and had developed a way to make the brain regenerate new cells in people who had developed brain damage. He spoke so technically that I thought that he must have been some kind of doctor. I noticed that his voice was very soft and smooth and he seemed to be speaking with some kind of a sing-songy accent. It was very slight. So slight, in fact, that I first thought that he was faking it for my benefit. I asked him where he was from and he told me that he was from Sweden. Actually, he said he was from "near Sweden." That didn't make much sense. It didn't sound like a Swedish accent to me, but what did I know? I found out later that he was, indeed, from somewhere other than the U.S. because he read to me out of a paper that was written in some foreign language. It was very sweet, the way he put his arm around me and laid the paper over our laps and read to me, having me repeat each word as he had spoken it in his language and then telling me what it meant in English. It reminded me of a father, reading the funny pages to his little girl. That's what I felt like; his little girl; his charge.

Throughout the entire trip, he was extremely protective of me. I don't think five minutes would go by before he would be asking me if I was okay or if I needed anything. In retrospect, I wonder how he knew I was in such need at that time? I don't believe what I was feeling inside showed much on the outside, especially to a stranger. I'm just too good at hiding my feelings. How did he know I was at a turning point in my life and was then probably more vulnerable than any other time in my whole life? Did he realize that he was acting as my guardian angel, or was it out of his control? Whatever the case may be, I will never forget his kindness, nor will I ever be able to thank him properly.

I noticed, after a while, that he never seemed to show any signs of beard growth, despite the fact that we were together for more than seventeen hours. I also noticed that every time he touched me, however lightly, on the arm, or face, his touch was exceptionally warm and I could feel that warmth flow through my whole body, relaxing and calming me. I didn't realize at the time how unusual any of this was.

Sometime in the middle of the night, the bus made an unscheduled stop. It appeared that Lars and I were the only ones awake on the whole bus. Wherever it was, it was pitch-black night and we couldn't see anything outside of the bus, except what was visible by the running lights on its sides. I saw the driver get off the bus and start to walk into the inky black the night. I wondered where he was going. If he had needed to use the restroom, there was one at the back of the bus, so why would he go outside to do that? Then, I wondered if he was checking something on the outside of bus itself. But why would he walk out into the night, and not around the bus? It just didn't make sense to me. I mentioned this to Lars and he told me not to worry about it. I bet we sat there for at least five minutes.

After the bus driver returned, we continued for a little while more. Then we stopped at an odd-looking truck stop/restaurant. By this time, I was the only one left awake on the bus. Even Lars had fallen asleep with his head on my shoulder. I had to crawl over him in order to get out of the bus. He was dead to the world. The bus driver followed me into the truck stop. I was hungry, so I went to where they were serving food. I noticed that the only people in the whole bus station were me, the driver, who had gotten himself a cup of coffee, and an old man and two girls. The old man and the two girls were working in the stop. And everyone was staring at me! I noticed they all had the same large, dark eyes that the bus driver had and their staring gave me the creeps. I shook it off as just being tired and worn out, both physically and mentally.

I purchased a sandwich and some orange juice. I thought that if I ate something, I'd feel better and things wouldn't creep me out so much. When I sat down to eat, I noticed that they were staring at me even more intently than ever. Boy, this was going to be a hard one to shake!

As I ate, I realized that the sandwich tasted just like the orange juice and had the texture of cardboard. But I was hungry, so I ate it. I looked up from time-to-time, to see the bus driver, the old man, and the two girls leaning against the wall, staring at me, still! They all had a funny kind of half-grin on their faces. "Oh, well, so they're weird," I thought. After all, what kind of life could someone have if they're working in a truck stop at two in the morning? (Nothing personal, mind you).

I finished up and then realized that I needed to go to the bathroom. I found my way back to the bathroom and thought it kind of strange that it was a "one-holer," since this was supposed to be a bus/truck stop/restaurant. I also thought to myself how unusual this building looked for a truck stop. It was kind of neat, rounded, and lined with panoramic windows.

When I went to wash my hands, I looked into the mirror. For a brief moment, I thought I could see not my own reflection, as I had expected, but the image of a tiny blonde girl whom I didn't recognize. She was wearing a cobalt blue, turtle neck top. "Whoa! What was in that crappy food, anyway?" I rubbed my eyes and looked again. Thank God, this time I saw the ugly mug I always see when I look in the mirror. It was time to get back on the bus, *now*!

As I passed by the old man, the girls and the bus driver, they all nodded at me. "Adios, weird people! Get a life!" I thought to myself. One lone passenger had stumbled off the bus while I was in the restroom. He passed me as I made my way back to the bus. He looked at me as if I were nuts and he was semi-comatose. He rubbed his eyes and shook his head, then turned around and boarded the bus right behind me.

Off we went, again. By this time, Lars had woken up. He had a funny grin on his face as he asked me where I had been and if I had enjoyed my snack. We continued our conversation.

Out of the blue, he blurted out that he wished he could dance with me right then. That was a strange thing to say, and yet, it meant something to me. At home, whenever I felt stressed out or just wanted to "let go," I would turn my stereo up real loud and dance my heart out. Music means a lot to me and when I dance, I "become" the music. It moves through me and *moves me*. It's not a pretty sight, but I really enjoy doing this. That's why I do it when I'm alone in the house. Often, I would get this unnerving feeling that someone was watching me, and that they didn't mind how I looked; they just wanted to dance with me. I got the feeling that they enjoyed my freedom of spirit when I did this. It may sound silly, but now, I found myself thinking, "You must be the one who dances with me." I was definitely not myself on this bus trip! As I thought of this, Lars just looked at me, and smiled.

At one point, he reached over to me, took my face in his hands and pulled my hair back over my ears. He said that this was the way women wore their hair where he came from and that I would look beautiful with my hair like this. Then, he asked me if he could kiss me. I said, "Okay." This was not like me, at all. I don't just kiss anybody, especially some stranger on a bus, for crying out loud! It was the softest, gentlest kiss I have ever had, and when he finished, he looked at me as if he had never kissed anyone in his whole life, and acted like he loved it. Believe me, I don't kiss any different from anyone else, and I'm sure I'm not that good! From the way he reacted you'd have thought I was Venus, the goddess of love, or something! From that point on, I think I was in some kind of trance or something, because I just don't kiss strangers. Hell, I don't even look at them, most of the time. On the trip to New York, I had never slept, and I'd sat there with my purse wrapped half way around my head to guard against strangers. The way I was behaving now was not *at all* like me, in any way.

We finally reached Columbus, Ohio, around dawn. Lars was to get off the bus and catch another one to Cincinnati after about an hour. I had a one-hour layover before my bus would leave for Indianapolis. We decided to go to the Burger King in the station and get something to eat for breakfast. When we started to order, Lars turned to me and asked me what the difference between bacon and sausage was. Then, he asked me what I suggested he should eat. I told him what the difference was between bacon and sausage. I told him both were good. He proceeded to order just about one of everything on the menu. When he saw how small the orange juice containers were, he complained, loudly, and then ordered four of them. The girls waiting on us looked at him as if he were some green-haired alien. I was kind of embarrassed by how weird he was acting, but one smile from him and I forgot all about that. I got my food and we sat down. As I looked at him, I found myself thinking, "I don't want to leave this guy! I don't know if I can live without him. Hell, I'll never see him again, and he doesn't even know my address or phone number." The moment this thought crossed my mind, he looked up at me with this startled look on his face, and then he smiled again, and he blurted out, through a mouthful of food, "Don't worry, we'll see each other again. Give me your address and phone number." He told me that there was a place near my home he wanted to take me to someday. It was a long, silver trailer and he would take me there to eat and dance. He couldn't promise when he would come back. It could be months or years, but he promised he'd be back to see me, someday. I believed him then, and I still do. I wouldn't be surprised if someday I get a knock on my front door, and it's him.

I said to him, "But, what if I move or something?" And he replied, "Don't worry, I'll find you." After we ate, we still had plenty of time before our buses were to leave so we decided to walk around the bus station. We passed a group of people sitting on the benches, who were dressed like old-fashioned Amish people. They absolutely stared a hole right through us as we walked by. I'd bet we were a sight—him so tall, and me so short—but the look we got from them was even stranger than just their noticing our height difference. They all looked totally dumfounded. I was talking to Lars when I noticed them. It was almost as if I were talking to *myself* and they thought I was some kind of nut.

I decided that I should use the bathroom before I left, so I told Lars that I was going to the restroom. "OK," he said, and, as I walked through the restroom door, he began to follow me in! I quickly pointed out to him that he shouldn't go in there, showing him the little international symbol for woman, on the door. I explained to him that the person with the skirt was female and then I pointed out the little man on the other door. I told him he should use the one with the little man on it, as he was a man. "Geez!" I thought, as I washed my hands.

When I pushed open the outer door of the restroom, I almost knocked him down. He had stood outside the door the whole time I was in there, making sure I was going to be okay, or perhaps to ensure that I would come back out again. No wonder no one came in while I was in there. He probably scared them off! As we continued our walk, he began to complain, "I have a funny feeling, right here." He was pointing to his stomach. I told him that his stomach was probably upset from all the crap that he'd eaten in the Burger King. I asked him if he felt nauseated. He asked me what that meant. I said, "You know, like you're going to puke, throw up?" He still didn't get it. I explained further, "That means that all the stuff you've put into your stomach, through your mouth, begins to come back up the tube and back out your mouth." I thought, "What a moron! Don't they barf in Sweden?" But I kept that to myself.

"Yes, that must be what I'm feeling," he said. I told him that I had some Pepto Bismal tablets in my purse and that he was welcome to a few, if he needed them. Of course, he didn't know what they were and he became very interested in them. I had to explain to him how they would coat his stomach to relieve his discomfort. I handed him a couple of tablets. He insisted on seeing the box and then proceeded to read each ingredient out loud, with great fascination. I was amazed. Then, instead of chewing them, he popped the tablets in his pocket. I told him they'd do him no good in there. He looked confused, and indicated that he'd take them later. There was a hint of embarrassment in his voice.

As we reached the end of the station, I noticed a row of newspaper boxes by the exit doors. He ran toward them and commented several times about how colorful our newspapers were. He asked me to buy him one. I did, and he took great delight in looking through it. Then, I heard the announcement that my bus would be soon boarding. My heart sank. I felt I would break out in tears at any moment. Lars walked me to the door and as I turned to board, he said to me, "When you get on the bus, look at the paper you bought for me, put your radio headphones on and listen to the music. You'll be okay now and remember, I'll never forget you and I'll see you again someday. This, I promise you from my heart."

I did just what he had instructed, and I cried my heart out as I did so. I couldn't believe that he was gone. I felt like I would die without him! What had he done to me? Why did I feel this way? If he had asked me to follow him to Cincinnati, I would have. Forget about my kids and my boyfriend. He was *it*. Boy, I really wasn't myself, at all!

When I turned on my radio, a song started, as if it were meant just for me: *This Much Is True*, by Spandau Ballet. I opened up the paper he had given me to a two-page ad about missing children. I looked at all those precious little faces, peering up from my lap. Then, I remembered my own two kids. I couldn't wait to get home. Those pictures were like a slap in the face, back to reality.

When I arrived at the station, my boyfriend and my kids were there to greet me. It was so good to see them again! I almost ate them up. But, in the back of my mind, was Lars. Later, after we got home, I told James about him. I told him everything. I didn't realize at the time how it hurt his feelings to see his girlfriend so worked up over some strange guy. He also pointed out to me how strange this guy sounded. I hadn't realized just *how* odd Lars' behavior really was. But you know, it didn't change how I felt about him. James persuaded me to call Budd and to tell him about my bus trip home.

I called Budd and he was absolutely fascinated by my tale of the trip. He was even more interested in how I had reacted to it, and how I was still reacting. I burst into tears every time I thought of Lars. I think I cried throughout our entire conversation. My heart ached for him; I longed to be with him again. Just to be near him would have been enough, and to hear his soft, sing-songy voice again. I really felt like I was going crazy. I used a little self-hypnosis to help me recall where it was Lars had told me he worked in Cincinnati, and, sure enough, I remembered! Budd took this bit of information and started digging. Miraculously, before too long, he actually found Lars. He was a real person, not some alien or angel. Thank God!

Budd had a lengthy conversation with Lars' childhood friend and discovered that all he had told me was true. He also unearthed a few other little bits of information. Apparently, Lars was a rather eccentric man, who was very fascinated by anything to do with the occult or paranormal phenomena, including UFOs. We also found out that he had been captivated by me during our time together and had talked about me constantly since he had returned home. His friend told Budd that Lars had a habit of taking off, sometimes for long periods of time, like for *years*, and no one would know where he was, or even if he was alive. Eventually, he would return, as if he had never been gone, with no mention as to where he had been all that time.

Budd gave me his friend's phone number and, as my heart pounded, I dialed it. I asked for Lars, and, a few moments later, I could once again hear that smooth, sweet voice. We had a nice talk and I told him I missed him. He reassured me that we would definitely meet again someday and that he had thought about me often since our trip, also. I got his address and told him that I wanted to send him something, a small token of my appreciation for his company during my trip home. I sent him a bronzed coin with two hands on it, clasped in friendship, and a little thank you note. He called me once more to tell me that he had received the gift, that he loved it, that he would keep it with him, always, and that every time he looked at it, he would think of me. That was the last I ever heard from Lars.

~

I have met a lot of strange people in my 60 plus years, but never have I ever met anyone like "Lars." Not too long after, I married my boyfriend and life went on. Although I have to admit that in the back of my mind, and for years afterwards, I *still* had a secret hope that I would someday see him again. So help me God, for *years* after, every time I heard a motorcycle, my heart would skip a beat and a little part of me would hope it was him, returning to take me to that "long silver trailer" to dance with me.

At that time, I was not as adept at computers as I am now. Back then, Google didn't exist. It wasn't until many years later that I began to search for him. I searched the Internet for his name and birthday dozens of times over the years. All I was ever able to find was an article or two from some obscure publication regarding someone with his name and age who raced motorcycles on ice. I assumed it had to be him (how many people with his name would actually do this?), and I knew this was something *he did* do, based on my conversations with him and on what his friend had told Budd. Of course, every photo I could find showed some guy on a motorcycle wearing a full helmet. That did me no good whatsoever. I felt like I was bashing my head against the same brick wall for years. Finally, I gave up. Motorcycles would rumble down my street with regularity, but he rode none of them.

Eventually, in around 2012, I started looking again. After all these years, he had resurfaced in my mind again. During an Internet search, I stumbled upon a small town in Sweden, on the coast, that suddenly rang a bell. I couldn't put my finger on it, and I do *not* recall him ever telling me *what* town he had lived in, but, for some reason, I was attracted to this town.

Then, I found a link to a cemetery. Something made me click on it. It looked like a lovely place. On the website, I found myself at a detailed map of graveyard and, eventually, I *found* his name! My heart dropped to the floor. The more I saw, the more I was convinced it was him. The birth date was correct. That was a detail that I had remembered for Budd when he was looking for him. And the date of death *really* knocked me off my chair. It was only about a year after we first met! I sat at my computer screen, just staring at the stark black letters that formed his name and I cried like a baby. In that moment, my heart hurt just like it did the day I left him in that Ohio bus stop.

This *had* to be him. All three names were correct; the birth date was exact. I was, and remain, convinced that this *is* his gravesite. I guess that would explain why he never came back for me, like he promised he would. Then again, perhaps he *did* visit me, albeit in my dreams...

I don't remember the exact date, but I know it was several years after I returned from my first trip to Budd's place in New York City when I met Lars on the bus trip home that I found myself admitted in the hospital with excruciating lower back pain. It was so bad that I had lost the ability to walk and I was receiving pain medication directly through an IV. The following morning, I was scheduled to have a myelogram on my lower spine—a procedure that uses a fluoroscope and a spinal injection to evaluate the spinal cord, nerve roots, and spinal lining. I was told that there was some real risk involved, but that it was needed to figure out what was going on, to alleviate the pain, and to get me on my feet again.

The night before my test, I had one of my vivid dreams. In this one, Lars came to see me in the hospital. I was surprised to see him because it was night-time, and visiting hours were over. Back then, hospitals were really strict about visitors. It was okay to smoke in your room, but you couldn't have a visitor after 8.00pm. Lord!

Back to my dream. When I first noticed he was in my room, he was standing near the window. You'd think he would have come through the door. But I didn't remember seeing him until he was by the window. He was wearing what looked like black leather jeans and a black leather jacket. All in black, from his top to his boots.

I was *so* happy to see him that I didn't even care how he got there. As soon as our eyes met, he broke out into a broad smile, just like he had done as he got on the bus that night. He came quickly to my bedside, and sat. He stroked my hair and looked at the IV in my arm; suddenly he looked upset. He asked me what kind of place this was. I told him this was called a hospital—a place where sick people come to get better. Then, I told him I was sick. I told him about my back and how much pain I was in, and that I couldn't walk. He leaned over and hugged me, tight. He whispered in my ear that I didn't belong in a place like this, and that I was going to be fine. He held me there for what seemed like forever. We didn't speak. He just hugged me and rubbed by head and back and feet. I fell asleep, and when I awoke he was gone and it was morning. I swung my legs over the edge of the bed, grabbed the IV pole with one free hand, the other clutching the open backed gown I was wearing, and headed to the bathroom. It wasn't until I sat on the toilet that I suddenly realized that I had just *walked* to the bathroom, and I had done it completely pain free! Once I finished my business, I pulled the call cord for the nurse to come. When she got there, the first thing she said was, "How in the world did you get to the bathroom by yourself?" (The day before, I was using a bedpan). With that, I stood up, straight as a board, and walked to my bed as though I was perfectly fine. Needless to say, the doctor was called, the test was cancelled, and, the following morning, I was discharged from hospital. I didn't tell anyone about my visit from "Lars," but I often wondered if my "dream" isn't what fixed my back. It had been so bad before I was admitted to the hospital that I was reduced to peeing into a bath towel on the floor because I couldn't stand up to get to the stool. That was when my parents finally had to call an ambulance for me. I had been in *very* bad shape. Whatever had happened, I was extremely grateful.

I had another dream about Lars a few weeks later. It was more of a memory-dream about that night he came to visit me when I was still in the hospital. By this time, I was pain free and off the meds, so I know it wasn't that. In the dream, it was just as I had remembered it from before, but this time, when he left, I had walked with him to the end of the hallway where my room was. We walked to the huge window. At that point, he hugged me again and told me he'd come back to see me, real soon, but that he had to go now. Suddenly he lifted up and passed right through the glass and out of the window, disappearing into the dark. Then I walked back to my room, got in my bed, and went back to sleep. Yeah, I know. Weird.

The last time I had a dream about him was a few years later. Again, this was one of those vivid dreams that I have, the ones where, the longer I'm awake, the more of them I remember and *never* forget. He just popped into my room, out of the blue. "Hey!" he said, "Wake up! I wanna take you somewhere and show you something so cool you won't believe it! Take my hand!" So, I did. As soon as I grabbed his hand, everything went black. I couldn't see a thing. Not even my own hand in front of my face. My room was gone; my *world* was gone! It was the blackest black I'd ever seen.

I could feel Lars' hand in mine, but his voice became suddenly distant. I felt weird. I felt *flat*. That is the only way I can think to describe this odd as hell feeling. *Flat.* I realized that I was suddenly unable to draw a breath, but yet I could "talk." I yelled to him, "Lars, I can't breathe! I feel *flat*! Something is wrong!" Again, I could feel his hand in mine, so I assumed he was right next to me. But I couldn't see anything. And his voice sounded almost like he was in another room. "*Oh shit!*" he said, "You can't go with me! You're not ready yet! *Shit! Shit!* We have to go back. Let go of my hand, *now!*" The second I let go of his hand, I sat straight up in bed, wide awake, out of breath and thinking, *what the fuck just happened here?*"

Years later, learning that "Lars" had passed away in 1987 made my "dreams" about him even more significant, because they all happened *after* he died. Maybe he *did* keep his promise, after all.

FOUR

Poltergeists and the Paranormal

~

For as long as I can remember, my family has almost continually experienced what some people would classify as poltergeist activity. We've experienced weird happenings in all of the places we've lived. When we moved into my parents' house, the activity noticeably increased. It's not so much the house, I think, because, no matter where any of us live—I in my new house, my sister in hers—it seems to follow us. But it would seem that something about my parents' place is exceptionally conducive to the phenomena.

One of my earliest memories of weirdness in that house dates from 1980, when I'd gone over there to do some laundry. Both of my children were very small—Rob about fifteen months old and Tommy only a couple months. Dad was working his first shift and Mom was at work in the local department store.

When I was alone in the house, as I was that day, I made a habit of locking myself in. If you could see where the house is located, you'd understand why. It's in the woods and appears to be way out in the country, but it's actually pretty close to a couple of local "dives" and other unsavory areas.

I had "camped out" in the basement recreation-room with the toddler in the playpen and the baby in his chair. As I sat there, folding towels and watching my soap opera, I heard the kitchen door upstairs open, followed by very heavy footsteps across the kitchen floor. Then, I heard several lighter sets of footsteps, following behind. I froze. A few minutes later, I heard the stereo in the upstairs living-room turn on and off, five times in a row. I freaked out. I was thinking about burglars, not aliens! I just sat there, holding my baby, listening intently, waiting for it to stop. After a few more minutes, it went quiet. Then, the baby started to fuss. He was hungry. *Oh great! Couldn't he wait till Grandma gets home?* I started to panic. I was truly terrified.

It was feeding time, and the rational choice was to feed the poor kid. I crawled up the stairs on my hands and knees. As I reached the slightly ajar door, I peeked around it and saw nothing. Taking a chance, I made a mad dash for the refrigerator. As I swung open the door, the lids on everything in the refrigerator—all of them—flew off and tumbled to the floor at my feet, including the baby bottle. I grabbed it, slammed the door behind me, and bolted back down the stairs, to the basement. This time, the baby would just have to drink his milk cold.

As I sat there, trying to feed Tommy the cold bottle, I began to hear footsteps, ascending and descending the upper stairs to the bedrooms. I decided to call my mother at work. I wanted to tell her what was going on, and to ask her what I should do. She told me to call my older sister. When I called Laura, she told me she thought that she'd heard someone pick up the extension upstairs and that they were listening to us talk. Now I was *really* panicked. I was beginning to feel like I was trapped in a really bad B-movie from which there was no escape. Laura told me to hang up, immediately, and call the police. So, I did.

After I talked to the dispatcher, I bundled up the babies and made my way out the basement door. By the time I got to the front of the house, the police were there. I took them back in through the same door I had come out from, because the rest of the house was still locked up. There must have been half-a-dozen police cars outside, and when the cops got out, their rifles were ready. They searched the grounds and then the house, thoroughly; they even looked in the attic. When nothing was found, they asked me when someone would be coming home. I told them that my father would be home by 3.30pm and that I thought I'd be okay until then. They told me they'd come back before then to check on us, and they did just that, twice.

I was surprised and relieved when I saw the cops drive by again to check on me and the boys. After the police came, nothing else happened that day. But that night, as my mother retold the story to my sister over the phone, she noticed that the interior light of the oven was on. This was strange, as she had never used the light in the oven, and no one would have had any reason to turn it on. It was confirmation for her that I was telling the truth—that something strange did indeed happen in the house earlier that day.

Many strange and ghostly happenings occurred in that house from then on. I would see things moving, out of the corner of my eyes. Often, if I would look fast enough, I could actually see a shadow slink away around a corner, leaving a sort of air distortion in its wake. Once, when my mother was in the basement, doing laundry, she noticed that one of the copper pipes that was lying across another had been twisted into a neat little knot, like a pretzel. While down in the basement, necking with a boyfriend, my little sister and her friend witnessed a coat-hanger that had been twisted around the door knobs of an old metal clothes cabinet untwist itself, and then the doors burst wide open, as if someone had kicked them from the inside out. This put a damper on the necking session, to say the least. She never could get that guy back in our basement again!

Objects had a way of disappearing, and then reappearing several days later in the strangest of places. We were beginning to think that all of this was some sort of test, as if someone wanted to see how supposedly rational people might react to irrational situations.

I had begun to date James by this time. He had given me a very nice "promise" ring to confirm our relationship. It meant the world to me. One morning, I awoke to find that the ring had vanished. I tore apart my room, trying to find it. I was devastated. I looked for that ring for three days and cried myself to sleep at night. During that time, I never told James that I'd lost the ring. On the third day, I was running the sweeper in the boys' room, when I was overcome by the feeling that I should look under Tommy's bed. I stopped the sweeper and looked under the bed. No ring. I resumed sweeping, and again I was hit with the feeling that the ring was under the bed. I looked again. This time, something was telling me that I was looking but not seeing, and to look *closer.* I moved the bed out from the wall. Running my hands over the carpeting, I suddenly had the idea to pull it up. I ran downstairs to fetch proper tools for the task, and, soon enough, I was ripping the carpet away from the baseboards. Then, up came the padding under the carpet.

By this time, my mother had heard the racket I was making and was stood there watching me. She was not too pleased with what she was seeing. But I wasn't about to give up. I felt that ring was *there*, even if I couldn't see it.

After a few minutes, I had the whole carpet, pad and all, up from the wooden floor and peeled back almost to the middle of the bedroom. There, on the wooden floor, about three feet from the baseboard, directly where the middle of Tommy's bed would be, was my beloved ring.

My mother watched in shock as I jumped for joy. It wasn't until later that night that I began to question how I could ever have known that ring was there. My mom was so flabbergasted that she stopped complaining about what I'd done to her carpet and called my sister to tell her about my miraculous find. Of course, I did fix what I had torn up, but, let me tell you, it's a lot harder to put carpet *back down*, than it is to rip it up!

One time, Mom and I were watching television in the living room with the kids. It was a clear night, about 8:00pm. All of a sudden, we heard a loud popping sound. At that very instant, I looked up and saw that mom and both the boys had covered their faces. There, in the middle of the living-room, was an incredibly bright green ball of light, about the size of a ping pong ball, approximately three feet from my mother's head and around three feet off the ground. It cast an eerie green light that illuminated the whole room. The bulb in the lamp blew and shattered, and the television switched off with a thump. I jumped off the chair and ran to the kitchen window—perhaps it was some kind of ball lightening—but all I could see were stars. The boys were crying and mom was mystified. It was several days before my kids would go upstairs by themselves; they wet their beds at night, too, and for several days following. I was just stunned. I had the willies for a few days. Later that night, mom asked daddy if a light bulb blowing out could cause such a thing to happen. He was an electrician, after all. He just looked at her like she was dense and said, "Not hardly." One more thing to record in my journal: around that same time, my mother and I witnessed a huge, boomerang-shaped craft pass right over our house and appear to light up, just for us (more on this one later, too).

On another occasion, my parents were awakened by the sound of someone beating on their front door at around 3:00am. It turned out to be the police. Several officers. My mother let them in and they explained that they'd received a phone call from our number and that it sounded like a woman who was in a great deal of distress. One of the officers told my parents that this woman sounded like she was trying to ask for help, and that she was wailing and crying so badly that they could barely understand her. Mom came up to my room and woke me. She asked me if I had called the police. I couldn't believe what she was telling me. As far as I knew, I had been in bed, sound asleep, all night.

As Mom explained to me what was happening, I could see her realization that I hadn't called the police any more than she had. I threw on some clothes and went downstairs with her while the police searched our whole house. At one point, they took my dad out to his workshop to check if someone may have broken in and phoned them from there. While they were out there, some of the other officers began intently questioning Mom and me. They were saying things like, "He's outside now. You will be safe if you tell us what's going on. He can't hear you now. You can tell us." Angered by their insinuation, my mom told the cop, "Look, there is really nothing going on here. We were all fast asleep when you came here, and my husband is *not* doing anything to any of us. Your computer must be on the fritz." With that, the officer had his dispatcher ring up the number their computer had locked onto. A few seconds later, the phone rang. He picked it up, said thanks to the guy on the other end, and hung up. Then, he came back to the table and leaned down. Speaking *real* low, he said, "The call came from that phone right over there. Are you ladies sure everything is okay here?"

After some serious convincing from my mom, the cops finally left and the three of us sat around the kitchen table with coffee and cigarettes, trying to figure out what the hell had just happened. "My God," I thought, "did I call the police in my sleep and not remember doing it? Did something weird happen here tonight and I can't remember it?" What an awful feeling it is to lose trust in yourself. Whether or not I did make that call, I guess we'll never know. Was this somehow connected to the phone calls I'd received when I was pregnant with my youngest son? I looked in the papers the next day to see if they might have found a woman lying dead by some phone booth, somewhere, but there was nothing. My parents speculated that either our "ghost" had made the call, or else the police computers were really screwed up.

We had another funny police story shortly after this happened.

We were all in bed, sound asleep, when suddenly we were awakened by what we thought were the screams of a frightened woman. Geeze, she sounded so close to our house, she could have been on top of it—and she *was*. Our screaming woman turned out to be the neighbor's pet peacock, trapped on our roof. Boy, did we feel like a bunch of dummies after calling this one in! I bet the guys downtown still talk about our family.

We would have another close encounter with Mother Nature shortly before the kids and I moved out, although this next one was far weirder, and more disturbing. We had a run-in with around five hundred bees who decided to visit my children's' bedroom one day. My oldest boy screamed for my mother to come up and see his room. He was using that "there *really is* something wrong" tone of scream, so we both raced up to him. When I looked into that room, I could not believe my eyes. There must have been at least five hundred bees in there, scattered all about. They were hanging from the curtains, clinging to the walls, all over the floor, and on both twin beds. They seemed very lethargic, almost in a stupor. I'd never seen so many bees in one place in my whole life. It was very creepy, like something out of a Hitchcock movie.

The first order of business was to get rid of the bees. We bombed the room with bug killer and, after they were dead, we began vacuuming and sweeping them away. Next, my father began looking for how they'd gotten into the room in the first place (we didn't want a repeat of this one!). He never could find where they'd made their entrance. We had no attic door, and the windows had been painted shut long ago. There was just no way for them to have gotten into that room. If it sounds like the *Amityville Horror*, that's sure what it looked like!

Even after I moved out of my parents' house and into my own apartment, weird stuff seemed to follow me and my boys. We were hit on the forehead by drops of water, seemingly from nowhere. I jokingly refer to these as our "baptisms." We've also had many encounters with small white balls of light that appear in our house and whiz past us, only to disappear before our very eyes. Many people who have been to our houses over the years have seen these little white lights. They are about the size of a marble, and you can almost feel static electricity as they pass by.

One night, the metal railings on the balconies of my building rattled so hard that my neighbors came screaming down to my apartment, thinking that we were having an earthquake. My neighbor, Brigitte, didn't know who I was or what kind of experiences I was having at that time in my life. One day, she told me about seeing six very small men in her bedroom, as she lay trying to sleep. This had happened long before she knew me. She said they wore pointed hoods and stood all around the foot of her bed, looking at her. I said that she should have told them, "Debbie's downstairs, you've got the wrong apartment!" She once commented to me that, "Nothing strange ever happened here until you moved in."

On another night, after my boyfriend James (soon to be my second husband) had moved in, he was awakened by the sound of glass breaking in the kitchen and what sounded like two-liter plastic bottles falling in the bathtub of our apartment. He got up to investigate, but found nothing. This sort of thing would continue over the years.

The first time I ever spent the night at the home of my third husband, K.O., while in the bathroom, I looked up to see the toilet paper roll unwinding itself onto the floor. I reached up to stop it and, when I let it go, it started again. I stopped it twice more before I left the room, pinching the cardboard tube to prevent it from moving. By the time it was done, it had unrolled nearly the whole way. I asked my husband if this happened all the time, because he had lived there all his life, and his grandparents before him. He couldn't believe what I was telling him. I thought it was pretty cool until I realized I would be the one to have to roll it back up.

On another occasion, as I stood in my hallway, talking to James, I saw a fuzzy creature the size of a large rat scurry down the wall from the ceiling and *pass through* the floor. I know that I wasn't the only one to see it because my cat pounced at it and began to dig at the spot where it went. It literally passed right through the floor and disappeared. I just shook my head. What was I supposed to do? I have never felt threatened or frightened by any of this strange stuff, just curious and sometimes amazed.

After having spent an evening in my neighbor's apartment and then going back to my own place to go to bed, I got a phone call from my neighbor demanding I tell her what was wrong. She claimed that she heard my voice coming through her window, calling her name as she was getting herself ready for bed. Apparently, I sounded like I was in need of assistance. I had no idea what my neighbor was talking about, but I reassured her that I was okay. *"Here we go again,"* I thought.

~

James was awakened one morning by a man standing at the foot of our bed. He was very tall, with stooped shoulders and long flailing arms. James' description of this guy reminded me very much of a man I had seen in the apartment before James had moved in, who had threatened to rape and murder me, but not before "I got what I deserved," whatever that means. I will discuss this experience in detail later on.

We have also been awakened in the middle of the night by the most putrid odors imaginable, wafting through the house. Whenever we try to investigate the odors, they dissipate as quickly as they appear. The smell is as if something has died, and is rotting. Imagine a combination of burning matches and rotten eggs—it's a smell that you can actually taste!

Our appliances turn on and off by themselves, and our answering machine has recorded itself calling other people's phone numbers. It's rather unnerving to check your messages, only to hear a phone dialing and then ringing. No one has ever answered these mystery calls but I'm curious as to exactly *whom* my machine could be calling. I worry that one day someone will answer in another country; I can't afford that sort of phone bill, and I doubt that the phone company would believe me if I blamed it on my answering machine!

Once, when my husband was working second shift, I had taken the boys to my mom's for the evening. When we came home, I was surprised to see the television on. I'm very good about making sure everything is turned off when I leave the house. As I walked over to the TV to turn it off, I noticed there were thumb tacks spread all over the oval rug on the living room floor. It looked as if someone had taken the time to turn each one point up and space them equally apart. I removed the booby trap tacks and proceeded to turn off the TV set. It was then I noticed that the VCR was also switched on and that there was a tape shoved into it, the wrong way. Obviously, it wouldn't work like this and I hoped it hadn't screwed up my VCR. When I pulled the tape out, I was shocked to see that the movie was *Close Encounters of the Third Kind*! I got chills. I don't know what all this poltergeist activity means, but I strongly believe that it is somehow connected to the UFO activity. It seemed that just before something UFO-ish happened, something paranormal would also occur, and both phenomena seemed to come together in cycles.

It still happens today. As I began to write the first chapter of the original version of this book, my computer took on a personality all of its own. After I had completed typing the "t" in the word "light," and was adding an exclamation point, my computer started beeping and began typing exclamation points all over the screen. This went on for at least three minutes, after which it stopped, backed up, and erased every one of the extra characters it had created. When it reached the point at which it had started, it stopped again, and I was able to resume typing. I tried everything I knew to stop this while it was happening. I even tried to turn the damn thing off; no such luck. So, I just sat there, arms crossed, watching, until it finished its little game. "Knock this shit off, will ya!" I said, out loud. And it did, just like that. When my then-husband, K.O., was transferring text that would become my manuscript from one diskette to another, it disappeared suddenly, and what appeared on the new diskette were programs completely unrelated my book. We had no idea how they ended up on that diskette. K.O. was an electrical engineer for 25 years for GM and he used computers for all that time, writing programs for GM's electronic equipment and products. He knew what he was doing. I could only assume it was my "friends," as my father called them, having a little fun with us.

My current husband, Dave, wasn't particularly interested in the world of UFOs or the paranormal, although he was open-minded. After he'd lived with me for a while, though, he became a believer in both.

My mother passed away in May of 2001, from lung cancer. When the cancer was discovered, Mom was told she was already stage-four and to get her affairs in order pretty soon. She was defiant and held on for another two-and-a-half years before she finally succumbed to it. She was strong up until the final week. She and I had talked a lot about death. She was raised a strict Pentecost and the doctrine was deeply ingrained in her, despite her being a rebel, marrying a Catholic Altar boy at 16 and not returning to church after that. She would often wonder aloud about death and God and Heaven, and if, when we die, we simply cease to exist. I used to tell her, "Well, if that is the case, you aren't gonna know, because you'll be dead, so it will be okay, I guess." One day, we made a deal, that when she passed over, if she was able, she would let me know, *somehow*, that there *is* something beyond death, that the body is just a vessel. She *promised*, and my mom never made a promise that she didn't keep.

She passed away at 11:30am in the morning. I was in the room with her, as were my older sister and my dad. When I realized she had gone, I fetched the nurse while my sister tended to Daddy. After the nurse confirmed that final heartbeat, I leaned down and whispered in Mom's ear that I loved her, that it was okay to let go, and to go into the light.

It was a very long day. I took Daddy back home and we stayed at the house for several hours, calling friends and family and gathering with my siblings. It was 11:00pm before I started that long-ass drive from my parents' place, back home to Kokomo, and it was probably the longest, loneliest, saddest drive of my life. I cried all the way home. By the time I arrived back at the house, I was completely exhausted. After talking to my husband for a few minutes and getting in the shower, I collapsed into bed. I think I was asleep before my head hit the pillow.

At approximately 1:30am in the morning, Dave and I were awakened from our sleep by something crashing and banging. Seriously, I almost peed the bed! The noise jolted me awake like a bolt of lightning, and I half-flung, half-rolled out of bed, onto the floor. Dave did the same.

Once we had got our bearings, we ran to the upper hallway and discovered what all the noise was about. We had multiple pictures of our kids and other family members, hanging on the walls of the stairway. One of the frames had fallen off the wall, rolled down the flight of stairs and was now *standing upright* at the bottom. It was a picture of *Mom*! I ran down the stairs, grabbed the picture and went back up to the spot where it had been hanging. The nail was still in the wall, and the hanging tab was still completely intact. It was as if someone had lifted the picture frame up off the nail and rolled it down the stairway.

I started shaking and yelling: "It's *Mom!* It's *Mom!*" Dave was kinda shook up; he followed me down to the kitchen to get a drink. I sat on the edge of the couch in the living room, trying to calm my dog, Cookie. She was panting and shaking, staring at the stairway.

I had three little angel figurines sitting on the edges of the steps that lead up to the first landing, where the picture frame had landed. I was calling out to Dave in the kitchen, insisting that picture was the sign that Mom had promised; I was *so* happy and excited, I could barely contain myself! At that moment, I looked up at the angels and was stunned to see the middle one literally lift up off the step and fling itself to the floor. It then rolled towards me, coming to a stop at my foot!

~

My step-daughter and I witnessed a blue ball of light entering our house through the kitchen window; it whizzed through the dining room, past both our heads, and back out the front window. Then, it made a U-turn on the front porch, came back in through the same window, went back through the house and out through the kitchen again. At that point, all I could say was, "Yup."

My step-daughter had never been a believer in weird phenomena. Not long prior to this, though, she had her own UFO sighting. She wrote her account for me, which I later posted on my blog:

On the morning of Friday March 17, 2009 at 5:30am, I woke up to my cell phone alarm clock and went to use the restroom. The blinds in the bathroom are almost always up since we live in the country and the bathroom faces the woods in the back. I caught a glance out the bathroom window and noticed a blinking bright light that kept moving around, really fast. I saw this same object about two weeks ago and told my parents about it. By the time I made it to their bedroom to wake them so they could see it, it was gone. This time, I happened to have my cell phone in hand because my alarm was not yet completely disarmed. I turned on my cell and video-recorded the UFO in the sky. I didn't think that it was going to show up since my cell doesn't record well in the dark. I tried it anyway. I opened the window to the bathroom so that I wouldn't get a glare. Once the window was opened I could hear noises that seemed as though they were coming from the UFO. It was like a humming, swirling buzz sound that would get louder then quiet, like it was going fast and slowing down. The neighbor's dogs were also barking and an airplane was flying right over the UFO. I couldn't guess how far away it was, because it was too dark outside for me to tell. The moon was to the right of the UFO and was easily triple the size of it. I caught several 30-second videos with my phone until the object got too far away to video with my cell phone. The UFO did show in the videos as a small white light and does show the movement I saw. I couldn't tell if the object had color to it or not. I thought I saw some rainbow coloring, but not for sure because it didn't stay in one place long enough to really focus in on it. Once my dad woke up I showed him the video. He went outside to check things out and didn't see anything. He told me to show the videos to my step-mom, so that she could analyze them. I was asked to write this report to explain what I saw. I have always been a skeptic until this incident.

～

One day, I had popped into the local Wal-Mart to pick up some stuff to make a salad for supper. As I was eyeing some pre-bagged salads, I started to feel strange, as if someone was looking at me. You know that feeling? I looked to my left, and there stood a very tall, slender guy with jet-black hair, black jacket and slacks, and very dark eyes. His skin was so pale and white that it made his eyes look even darker, like they were jumping out of his head and into my mind. It was creepy. Creepier still was the odd, "Cheshire Cat" grin on this guy's face as he stared at me. I still shudder when I think about it. It felt almost like time had stopped. I was so startled that I looked away for a brief moment and, when I looked back, he was gone! I literally ran to the end of the aisle to see if I could catch sight of him again. It had only been a second or two—he couldn't have gotten far. But there was no sign of him. I ran all over that store, frantically. I *needed* to see this guy again, so I could believe my own eyes. I searched the entire store. He was *nowhere* to be found. It took me a few days to shake that creepy feeling. I have *no* idea what it was all about. Maybe it was just a test, to see if I could see him. I really don't know.

Back in about 2008/2009, when I was working at my job on the factory production line, I experienced a strange phenomenon with time. I have had sensations, in the past, where, right before or during a strange event, such as the one above, time felt *different*. Sometimes, it would feel as if the world was speeding up and I was slowing down, or vice-versa, and I'd have to hang on to something to stay with it. It is certainly not the same sensation as feeling dizzy or faint. It is noticeably different.

I had what I thought was another vivid dream a few years ago, around 2016/2017. In the dream, I was sitting in my dining room, at the table, drinking a cup of coffee and reading the paper. Suddenly, I felt someone looking at me. I peered up, and in front of my son's closed bedroom door, hovering up on the corner by the ceiling, was this *thing*. It was a white sheet-looking-thing, but it had two eyeholes cut out of it. The eyeholes were black. The sheet was waving and it looked like it was draped over a human body. And, get this; there was a pair of black and white Hi-Top Chuck Taylor shoes hanging out the bottom! Who the hell sees Casper the friendly ghost hanging around in their hallway, staring at them while wearing Hi-Top Chuck Taylors? *Me!* That's who!

Honestly, I was startled at first. I could feel that jolt of adrenaline but as soon as I saw those shoes, I burst out laughing. And it was weird because I suddenly got a strong feeling that this was exactly the intended response—that it (whatever "it" was) wanted to get my attention but didn't want me to be afraid. I felt like it was trying to communicate something to me, but, honestly, I never did figure out what it was. The moment I started to laugh, and said out loud, *"What the fresh hell?"* he was gone.

When I awoke the next morning, I remembered the entire dream and wrote it down right away. I was sitting at my kitchen table, drinking coffee and reading the paper, when my son flung open his bedroom door and yelled, *"Mom!* You won't believe what happened last night!" He then proceeded to tell me that, while he was lying in his bed, he opened his eyes and saw someone looking into his bedroom window. At first, he pulled the covers up over his head, but then he decided to get up and see who it was. My son said that, whoever it was, they were tall as hell, because their head reached up to the top of the window frame. I thought it was pretty strange that, at the same time I was having my weird dream about being watched, my son was having one of his own—and the height of my son's "observer" would actually have been about as high up in the house as "Casper" was. We went outside to see if there were any footprints in the soft dirt in front of his window, but there were none. My son swears that someone was there. He was quite agitated when he was telling me.

I felt more drawn to the paranormal side of things as the years passed. After I had my hysterectomy, and then my late husband passed away, I didn't have any major UFO experiences for quite a while. Things got really quiet. It was almost as if the phenomena themselves realized I needed a break.

I became very interested in something called EVPs, or Electronic Voice Phenomena—disembodied voices or sounds captured in recordings that are interpreted by some as voices from other realms. EVPs can be captured unintentionally or intentionally, on tape or digital recorders. I had dabbled with EVPs in the past and decided to look into local paranormal groups, to expand my horizons, so to speak. I met with a group based in Indianapolis, about 50 miles south of me, and quickly became an official member. It was around this time that I began getting back into UFO investigations. I am proud to say that I was the one who introduced Indiana MUFON to the paranormal group I was working with. Together, these two groups collaborated on several cases and my gut feeling that there was a connection between UFOs and other paranormal phenomena was getting stronger and stronger. By the time I left both groups and started out on my own as a freelancer, the only common denominator I could identify was the experiencer themself. But that only led to a hundred *new* questions that are still begging to be answered. This should keep me busy well into my eighties!

It was around this time that I co-hosted a podcast, Midwest Paratalk Radio, with my friend, Greg Cable. It ran for several years. I had a ton of fun with it, and Greg and I had great chemistry. Unfortunately, when our day jobs moved out of state, our location started to interfere with our broadcasting schedule and eventually we had to shut it down. It was fun while it lasted and I learned a lot about the world of the paranormal during that time. I really did love being a radio host, and I hope that someday I can do it again. I have the perfect face for radio!

FIVE

Government Involvement?

~

S hortly after my family began communicating with Budd, strange
things started to happen.

One Sunday afternoon, I got a call from Joyce Lloyd, our neighbor
to the north. She and I had become friendly. She had been a witness to the
night of June 30, 1983—a fact uncovered by Budd during his investigation.

When Joyce called, she expressed concern at the fact that she had
seen a strange man in our backyard the day before. She had described
him as middle aged, dressed in a business suit and tie, carrying a large
briefcase and driving a dark colored sedan. Joyce said that when the
man reached the mark in our backyard, he set his case down, opened it,
and did something to the ground in that area. She could not see what,
exactly, as his back was to her for part of the time.

When the man was done, he quickly packed up his stuff and left.
We had not been at home the day the man appeared. Likely it was
planned that way.

My family would often sit at the kitchen table and watch the wildlife
in our back yard. On several occasions, while my mother and I were
sitting at the table, someone in an older model car would pull up,
jump out of the car and proceed to snap several pictures of the back of
our house and of the mark in the yard. The people I witnessed didn't
look like government agents to me. As a matter of fact, they looked
downright grungy. You have to remember, though, at this point in the
investigation, no one knew who we were, or where we lived. The book
hadn't been written yet and Budd had not gone public with the case.
Who *were* these guys?

On other occasions, my father and I have both witnessed large black vans pull up alongside the road in front of my parents' house. We've watched several men exiting these vans and climbing the telephone poles in front of the house. They were not from the phone company. We are sure of that because we checked with the phone company. My father approached them once and was told to mind his own business before they abruptly left the scene. They must have assumed that their activities were obscured by the row of trees that borders my parents' property. If so, they thought wrong. Nothing slipped past the Old Man.

The day after I moved into my house, I began having problems with my phone. I'd pick it up and the line would be dead. The next minute the phone would ring; when we would answer it, there would be no one on the other end. The next day, I received approximately 30 "dead" phone calls, with only silence from the other end.

Up until my life-changing incident of June 30, 1983, not one of us had ever seen a black helicopter. After that fateful experience, however, we were to see them nearly every day for almost five years. They would fly over our house, below 1000ft.—*well below*—three or four times a day. Whenever my close family were travelling by car, a black helicopter would appear in close proximity, following us wherever we went. Sometimes, they would come in formation, five of them. Sometimes, they would be so close that if their windows weren't tinted, we could have told you the pilot's hair color. One of these black helicopters came so close to my sister's car one time that she was almost run off the road. She told me that if it had been any closer, she could have reached out her car window and touched the damn thing.

One evening, a black helicopter flew circles around my house for over an hour. The pilot, whoever he was, made more than 45 passes of my house. Each time he made his approach, he would turn on this high-speed strobe light and direct it toward my windows. As soon as he made his pass, he would shut off the strobe until his next approach. He was so close to our house that the noise cracked my bedroom window. My neighbors were calling, asking me what was happening—they thought the helicopter was the police and were concerned that something was wrong at our house.

It got worse. My children were playing in the field next to our house with several of the neighbors' kids when I had heard a helicopter coming around. When I went outside to bring them in, they met me halfway, screaming at the top of their lungs! All at once, they proceeded to tell me the same story. They told me that a black helicopter had flown so close to them that it had stirred up dirt in the field—that a door opened on the side of the helicopter and that a man had leaned out with some kind of camera on his shoulder. They thought he was taking pictures of them. They said he picked up some kind of instrument and began talking to them. He asked them if they wanted to go for a ride. This is when they came screaming home. These kids were genuinely frightened and it took several minutes for me to get them calmed down. My oldest boy and his oldest friend both said that the man was wearing a dark green jump suit of some kind and that he had blond—really blond—hair. Boy, was I mad! Messing with me is one thing, but messing with my kids is something else. But what could I do? Who could I call and complain to? I called Indianapolis International Airport and asked who might be doing it. They said they had no idea, but suggested I call Fort Harrison, a local military installation. Perhaps they were coming from there.

That's when I had the idea to turn the tables. When next I was followed by a black helicopter, I followed it back, and, sure enough, it led me straight to Fort Harrison, but I was afraid to get any closer. So, when he started to land, I left.

One of these things even landed on the front lawn of the high school where I used to work. I was coming back from taking my oldest son, Robby, to a doctor's appointment. As we were going down the street where the school was situated, he yelled at me, "*Mom!* There's a helicopter like the one that talked to us that day!" I nearly skidded off the road. Sure enough, there it was, sitting on the ground, surrounded by Army guys, who looked as if they were guarding it. Later that afternoon I heard on the TV news that something had gone down in the woods next to Fort Harrison and that they were searching for it. People had reported hearing voices calling for help in the woods, but nothing could be seen. The news showed Army men in full combat gear, with guns, marching through the woods, searching for the object. Some people reported seeing a fireball coming down from the sky; they were told that it was probably a helicopter, but they said in response, "No way, I know what a helicopter looks like and this wasn't a helicopter." I wondered if they hadn't put the black helicopter down at the school as a cover. They never did report what they found, except to say that there was no sign of wreckage and that they had no idea where the calls for help had come from. I heard someone say that it sounded as if you were standing right next to them, yet could see nothing. This all happened within five miles of my house.

~

On one occasion, I was sitting in my living room, watching my soap opera on TV. It was a nice, quiet day; all the work was done and the kids would be home from school soon. I was enjoying one last hour of peace and quiet. There was a knock on my screen door. I was surprised to see a very nice-looking man standing outside. I don't know why, but I invited him in. I noticed that he was driving a brand-new car. Very nice. He sat down and told me that Budd had given him my address. My little red flag went up. Budd wouldn't do this without telling me first.

"Oh, well," I thought, "Let's just see what he wants." He began to ask me about the feeling I sometimes had before I went to sleep, before something weird happens—that paralyzed feeling. Only, he stated it wrong; it actually happened to me right before I wake up, not before I go to sleep. I corrected him, but I got the feeling that he was testing me in some way. That was all he wanted to know about. He thanked me for my time and for letting him into my home. He said if he had any more questions, he'd be back. Then, he left. How weird. Of all the things that have been written about me, you'd think he'd have more questions than that, especially having gone to the trouble of finding me.

I received a phone call from a man who claimed to be a journalist from Washington, D.C. He claimed that they—whoever "they" were—were interested in the phone calls I had received when I was pregnant with my second son. They said they had found out where the calls were coming from—somewhere in outer space! He said something about going to a "protected area" there in Washington D.C. for some kind of meeting. He also claimed to have gotten my phone number from Budd, but that Budd had given him the wrong one, yet he found me anyway.

My neighbor, Brigitte, called me and said that this man had somehow gotten the phone number of an old neighbor of mine, Rhonda, and that he had drilled Rhonda for my phone number.

Rhonda's phone number was listed, but Brigitte's was not listed with an address. Why did he call these two old neighbors of mine in order to get my number, and how did he figure out they were my neighbors? What was so important that he had to get a hold of me, anyway? I never did figure out what the hell he was trying to tell me, and I never heard from him again. Good. Probably a nut, rather than a government man.

The last thing I want to mention here, in regard to possible government involvement, is a memory I have of something that happened one night in 1986. I can't say for a fact that this really happened. It may be some kind of screen memory. I have never been able to find the man I was with that night to ask him. He disappeared after he took me home the next day. It's an interesting story, though, so take it for what it's worth.

A man I'll call Dave was coming to pick me up and take me to his cabin in the woods for a romantic weekend—just the two of us. I had been introduced to him a few months earlier, by my best girl friend. She worked with him at a large factory in Indianapolis. From the moment we met, he couldn't keep his hands off me. He was crazier about me than I was about him. But I was giving him the benefit of the doubt, as I figured that I just wasn't used to getting that much attention from a man and that this might be good for me if I could just get used to it. He seemed to like my kids really well and he was financially secure, so, I thought, "What the hell. I'm not getting any younger or prettier or skinnier."

When he invited me for a romantic weekend, I had mixed feelings, but I thought maybe it was just what I needed to get accustomed to his affections. I had been seeing him for several months and certainly I trusted him enough to know that I'd be safe.

When we arrived at his cabin, I remembered getting out of his car and thinking that I saw someone dart behind a bush, next to the drive. I remember saying, "Hey, Dave, I think someone is snooping around your cabin!" As he got out of his car, the look on his face changed to pure terror. The next thing I remembered was seeing something go over my face, turning everything black and feeling a sting on my right arm.

I remember coming to, still unable to see, but feeling as if I were moving and hearing the sound of an engine. Then, I blacked out again, before briefly coming to once more and feeling as if I were descending in an elevator. Then, I was out cold. In my next memory, I can actually see what's happening in front of me. I'm being stood up and forced to walk down a long white hall. I notice white tiling and a chrome-like bar running along the wall, half way up. The windows we pass have little wires running crisscross through the glass. I'm surrounded by six men—humans—wearing orange jump suits and orange ball caps. They're all around the same height and build, much taller than my 5'4." Ahead of us are two men in white coats—older men with deep voices and very thick southern accents. I'm no longer in my clothes, but I'm wearing some kind of hospital gown and paper booties. I don't want to be here, and yet, somehow, I cannot resist them. I'm in a daze.

They take me to a room with glass walls. In order to get into the room, one of the two men in white coats has to put a little card into a slot at the right side of the door and speak an entry word. The doors swing open and outward to create a huge entrance.

They put me on a table and proceed to take samples—blood and skin and mucus—from every opening of my body. They also give me several shots of something. I just sit there and let them do everything. I can't fight. While I'm sitting there letting them do this to me, I notice that the room I'm in is actually a smaller part of a much bigger room. This huge room is divided into smaller rooms with glass walls. Huge sliding doors connect the rooms together. In these other rooms, I can see other tables, just like the one I'm on. Fortunately, I can't see anyone else in there like me.

The older man in the white coat—I call him the Doctor—gets up real close to my face and says to me, in a deep southern drawl, "Honey, you've got a bug in your ear and I'm gonna take it out for you right now. It won't hurt and you'll feel a lot better after I finish." Then, he sticks this long, shiny metal instrument in my ear. It hurts. When he pulls it out, he shows me what he's gotten out of my ear.

When I first look at the little ball, it resembles a mosquito, all crusty, with its legs and wings out. Then, as he tells me to look at that bug, it begins to look like a b-b, all bloody and crusty. The legs and wings disappear. Then he says something else to me—something I can't remember. With that, he looks at me, smiling, and says, "Well, I don't know why I'm even bothering to tell you this. You're not going to remember any of this anyway." I look up at him and say, in my dopey state, "Oh yes I will. I'll never forget you, not as long as I live." He laughs at me... and then I black out again.

~

Next thing I remembered, I was in Dave's cabin, waking up on his sofa sleeper. I looked up and saw Dave's emergency monitor flashing in the corner of his room. Dave's an EMT, so he keeps it on all the time. I went back to sleep.

The next morning, Dave took me home. I was supposed to have stayed the whole weekend, but Dave changed his mind and decided to take me home, right then. He hardly spoke two words to me the whole way home and after he dropped me off that day, I never heard from him again. I felt awful on the trip home, physically and emotionally. I kept thinking that something had happened the night before, but I just couldn't remember what it was.

When I got home, I lay on the couch and tried to get some rest. I felt as if I had a terrible hangover, but I don't drink. As I lay there, drifting in and out, I began to remember the story I just told you. The longer I lay there, the more I remembered. By the end of the day I had remembered it all and I was really upset. Who was I going tell? Who would believe me? I tried to call Dave, but I never did manage reach him. Eventually, I told Budd about this, but he didn't know what to make of it, so it went in the peripheral file, to be explored later. I never forgot it, though.

Several years later, my friend ran into Dave at the plant she worked in. He asked if I was okay. That was all he said about me. She told me that he had sold his cabin, grown a beard, transferred jobs and gotten married. She said he seemed nervous and concerned when he asked about me.

A couple of years after this, I gave a talk to a MUFON group about my experiences and how they've changed me. During my lecture, I noticed two men sitting in the front row. Both had on dark suits and ties. One guy was even wearing sunglasses—*inside.*

As I presented my talk to the MUFON group and shared technical details from my memories, one of the men jumped up and asked me if the mark in my yard ever had a funny smell about it. I told him yes, it did. My answer seemed to satisfy the two men, as they then immediately stood up and left the building.

I began to feel strange after that little interaction, and was glad when my talk was finally over. I really wanted to get out of there. I asked the group organizers who those two guys were. They didn't know, but, apparently, they showed up from time to time, whenever the group hosted a controversial speaker.

As I made my way back to my hotel room, I suddenly began to realize why these men had bothered me so much. The one who had questioned me looked and sounded just like the doctor I had remembered taking the bug out of my ear, years earlier. If it wasn't him, he's definitely got a twin. The man was in his fifties, about 5'8" or 5'9," and weighed about 200lbs. He had a really red-looking face, a big, bulbous nose and snow-white hair. He had the deepest voice

I have ever heard and he had a very prominent southern drawl. He also had really blue, squinty eyes.

I'm just telling you what I remember. I'm not saying I know what it all means. Maybe someone reading this can shed some light on it for me.

SIX

It Gets Weirder

~

On April 24, 1984, I had the most unusual UFO sighting of my life. I was giving myself a manicure that evening when I found that I had run out of nail polish remover. For some reason, I decided that I had to go out and get some more, even though it was getting rather late and I could have waited until the next day. I hopped in my car and ran down to the all-night convenience store on the corner. On the way home, heading south on our street, I saw what looked like the landing lights of a very large jetliner. I watched the lights for a moment. When I reached the railroad tracks a quarter mile or so north of our driveway, I stopped to get a better look.

As I sat there at the railroad tracks, I observed two exceptionally bright lights slowly move together to form a single, intensely bright light. I couldn't believe my eyes. I floored the accelerator and raced home. I burst through the front door, yelling like a crazy woman for mom to come out and see this thing. It was headed right for our house! She came outside, calmly, and looked up. "Debbie, that's just an airplane," she said. But I knew it was no ordinary airplane. I told her to wait a minute and she'd see what I meant. We stood on the front porch for three or four minutes. We could see the thing coming toward us through the trees. The bright light looked eerie as it shone through the half-bare branches above our heads. As it reached the clearing right above our house, it was obvious that this was no normal aircraft.

It was moving extremely slowly, like a dirigible, and its wingspan was huge. It covered the whole clearing in the trees above us. It looked to be around twice the length of our house, a bedrock tri-level. I don't know of any plane that can fly so slowly at such a low altitude—approximately 200 feet—and not fall out of the sky.

We noticed a slight humming sound as it got closer to us, and yet the sound grew no louder at all as it began to pass overhead. It was shaped like a boomerang. Up in the front where the two wings met, there seemed to be a round, dark area. Inside this dark area was a pulsing red light. I could also see a dark area behind the wings that looked rectangular, with a long, pointed protrusion off the back, giving it the vague appearance of a stingray.

As we stood there looking at this thing, it suddenly lit up! At this point, it was directly above us and the whole underside came alive with an audible "womp." I could see many, many small white balls of light, dotted all over the bottom of this thing, and several long strips of light—like luminous tubes—bordering the edge of the two wings. It was striking, to say the least. The rectangular rear remained dark; only the wings lit up. My mother exclaimed how beautiful it was and stood there on the porch with her mouth agape. She remarked that it seemed to have lit up "just for us."

I, on the other hand, was rather less enchanted. All I can remember thinking to myself was, "Oh shit, here we go again!" I was not mesmerized, as my mother was. I was terrified. I grabbed hold of the screen door and stood there, one foot on the porch, one foot in the house. As the craft passed over us I ran inside through the kitchen and out the back door—I wanted to keep my eye on this thing. I wanted to know where it was at all times. I wasn't about to let it sneak up on me (incidentally, I was so out of my mind with fear that I ran right past a loaded camera that was sitting on the desk right by the front door).

I watched it pass over the house and then, when it was around half-a-mile away, I saw it turn on its axis, spinning around to face the opposite direction, and travel back to the southwest. I couldn't believe what I was seeing. No airplane can do that! I watched it until it was out of sight.

Immediately, Mom and I began to draw what we had seen. When Dad got home from work later that evening, we nearly knocked him down in our rush to tell him what he'd missed. He suggested we call someone to report this thing. I'd received some literature from Budd about CUFOS—one of the best-known and most reputable UFO research groups in the country—so I dug out one of their journals and called the UFO hotline number. Dr. J. Allen Hynek answered the phone. I was rather surprised by this. It was around 11:00pm. Rather late, I thought, for Dr. Hynek to be awake. Our sighting had occurred at around 9:30pm.

We talked for about an hour and we agreed to send him our drawings. Dr. Hynek talked with both of us on the phone, independently. He told my mother that he was beginning to believe that only certain people were meant to witness these events.

We noticed there were no UFO sightings of any kind reported on the radio or television that night, or any night after that. This surprised us because the craft was huge and we found it hard to believe that no one else had seen it. I look at this event as just further confirmation of my previous experiences—confirmation that I really didn't need.

By February of 1986, I was nearly ready to move out of my parents' home and to begin my own life with my two boys. I was dating the man who would soon become my second husband—James. I had completed beauty school with excellent grades, and I was working at my first job in the field. Life seemed to be settling down for me. Unusual things were still happening but I guess I was slowly becoming accustomed to them, or, at least, they didn't seem to frighten me quite so much as they used to.

One night that year (I don't recall the date), I was in my room watching television when my oldest son ran into my room acting very frightened and upset. He claimed that there was a scary "red spider" on his wall. He wanted to get into bed with me so he'd feel safe. I had gotten used to this by now so I had him lie down on my bed, and I covered him up as I sat across the foot of my bed, watching TV. I figured he'd had a bad dream so I didn't bother to look for the red spider. In hindsight, it seems the red light on his wall may somehow have been connected to the phenomenon.

As I sat there, watching TV, I was absolutely stunned to see a blue light appear at the far edge of my bedroom doorway. As I continued to look, I saw—with both eyes wide open—the luminous blue outline of a grey alien type-figure strolling past my bedroom door. I sat there with my mouth wide open in total shock. He walked past my door and into what I will describe as an invisible doorway that began just before he got out of my field of vision. By this time, he appeared blue and somewhat transparent. As he walked by my doorway he momentarily turned his head towards me, as if to balance himself while he walked. I got the distinct impression that he either was not aware that I could see him, or he just didn't care if I could.

As he passed through this invisible doorway, wherever his outline touched or passed through it, it created tiny sparks that reminded me of Fourth of July sparklers. As soon as he passed all the way through, he was gone—and so were the sparks.

I sat there for a moment, trying to comprehend what I had just witnessed. Looking at my son lying there, fast asleep, I thanked God that he didn't see what I had just seen. How could I ever explain *this* one away? Also, I felt guilty because I hadn't gotten up to investigate the red spider. I was sure by now that it was connected to what I had just witnessed. This thing appeared to come from the direction of the boys' room. I was terrified and angry at the thought of this creature hurting and scaring my children.

I don't know how long I sat there on the edge of my bed trying to regain my composure. I recall hearing a slight humming sound coming from outside my bedroom window, but I wasn't about to look out there after what I'd just witnessed. When I could finally get off the bed, I jumped up and ran to my parents' room. I insisted they get up and I begged mom to lend me the money to rent a hotel room. She knew I was serious, so she did as I asked. She made a pot of coffee and we sat there at the kitchen table for nearly forty-five minutes as I told her the details of what I had just witnessed. No amount of coffee and cigarettes could calm me down. Finally, I went back to bed, this time with both of my boys so I could watch and protect them. I didn't sleep that night.

~

All throughout this time in my life I had been writing down everything that I could remember about my strange experiences. These were consciously recalled memories, not retrieved through hypnosis. I created collages and pencil drawings of images I remembered seeing on the craft, as well as what looked like writing of some unknown origin. I thought perhaps these things might be of some importance to someone, someday. In any case, if I didn't write them down, it ate away at me; I couldn't rest. I found it therapeutic. After a couple of years, I had collected quite the stack of material.

I gave a lot of this material to Budd. By this point, though, there was just so much information that he decided to hold a lot of it back, so as not to confuse his prospective readers. I have always felt that the fact that I was remembering this information was important, even though the material itself might not mean anything. I think Budd felt the same way, although he was already becoming overwhelmed by the magnitude of our case and didn't know quite what to do with it all. I truly felt sorry for him!

It was during this time that I had begun to collect seeds from the various plant life around my home. It became an obsession for me and

I distinctly remember getting anxious for the time when the buckeyes would begin to fall from the trees. I needed to add them to my collection.

After a few months of this, my room was starting to look like a horticulturist's dream. I had seeds from just about every type of plant life known in the Midwest. I was proudest of my cattails, which turned out to be the hardest specimen to collect. What a pain in the rear it was to pull over to the side of roads and climb through muddy, swampy ravines to retrieve my prize. I'm sure I looked like a total nut! My reasoning was this: I wanted to have a little piece of this world as it was at this time, so that, if it all changed one day, I would have at least some natural part of it to show my children, so that they would know what it was like. I feel a very close attachment to nature to this day, although the compulsion to collect specimens of it has stopped.

Actually, it stopped quite abruptly one morning. I woke up to see that just about everything I had collected was now gone from my room, overnight. Even my prized cattails were gone. I panicked and immediately accused my younger sister of taking them. She had been lusting after my cattails for a flower arrangement she was making. She was surprised when I asked her to please return my stuff, and she denied having taken them. I never saw any of my collection again, and, after that day, my desire—my drive—to collect them, stopped forever. After I moved out of my parents' house and into an apartment of my own, I figured that all this craziness would stop. It didn't.

One night, after my first husband had picked up the children for the weekend, I decided to take advantage of the quiet time by mopping the floors of my apartment. While I was mopping the floor near the patio door I heard a faint beeping sound. It sounded like someone's watch alarm. I stopped what I was doing to listen and see if I could figure out where it was coming from, but I couldn't, and so I continued to mop. By the time I was finished, I was completely worn out. At that time, I was sleeping on an old army cot that a girl friend had loaned me (I had previously been sleeping on the floor, and so even this was an improvement). I lay down on the cot, hoping sleep would come quickly.

As I lay there, trying to relax, I noticed, through the open bedroom door, some movement in the living room. I could see my rocking chair moving and I could hear the rustle of leaves from one of my large potted plants. At first, I thought it must have been one of the kids, but then I remembered that they were with their father. I became nervous, so I got up and closed and locked my bedroom door. It seemed to be quiet for a while after that, so I began to drift asleep. Then I started to hear voices speaking in some foreign language. I also heard a rather loud banging noise coming from the living room. I sat up in my bed only to see a very scary, ugly man burst through my bedroom door, lunging at me. Tall and skinny, he had very short hair, very pointed, yellowed teeth and evil yellow eyes. His arms were long and spindly and he was waving them around wildly. He held in his hand a long, triangular shaped stick that he kept poking at me. He was cursing at me, screaming that he would kill me, but not before I got what was coming to me, whatever that meant. I somehow felt that he meant to rape and beat me before he would finally let me die. He kept poking at me with that stick until he had poked me right into the corner of my room.

There I sat, curled up in a little ball on the edge of my cot, practically smashed into the corner of the two walls, while this guy that I would later refer to as "the rubber band man" threatened to kill me. It was like a nightmare, but it seemed too real! Suddenly, it dawned on me. I was going to die. This guy really was going to kill me. I panicked and started to black out. Then, from out of nowhere came the beeping sounds again—the ones I'd heard earlier in the evening while mopping the floor. As soon as the rubber band man heard the sounds, he freaked out. He began writhing in pain before turning and bolting out of my room. I jumped off the cot and started after him. I was dumbfounded as I watched him run through the sliding glass door—literally *through* it! I opened it up and went out onto the patio to see where he had gone.

The next memory I had after that was being on what looked to me to be some kind of huge bus. I was sitting in front of a whole lot of big, long windows, through which I could see two strange-looking ships outside, with my apartment building down below. These ships looked like stick insects—sort of like an airplane with several sets of real skinny wings that were bent down, halfway out from the body. Then clouds of some kind—mist perhaps—started to surround the two ships and obscure them from my view. Then, a few minutes later—as the mist dissipated—they were gone. I heard a voice, from out of nowhere. It told me that this had been a test. "Do not be afraid, you are safe," it said. That's the last thing I remembered about this whole event. I've no idea what it meant, if anything.

~

On May 15, 1987, I married my boyfriend, James. He had been through so much with me by this point that I figured he really must love me, so

I shouldn't let this one get away. He knew what kind of person I was and he had seen enough to know that I wasn't as crazy as I might sound to someone who hadn't been there. I was thrilled to have had him in my life and so we took the "big dance."

On the evening of October 31, 1987 (Halloween, appropriately enough), I returned home from my shift at the convenience store next to my apartment building. I was tired and ready for bed, despite still being wound up from work and all the coffee and cigarettes I'd consumed. James was already asleep in bed as I slipped in next to him and began to relax. My mind was going over the day's events and I was almost ready to drift off when suddenly I experienced what I call a "brain shock." My mind was filled with what looked like the luminous snow you see on a blank television screen. In my mind I could "see" wavy, horizontal lines and I could "hear" a very loud, uncomfortable hissing sound.

At first, I thought I was having a stroke. I took a mental assessment of all my extremities and when I had finally determined that I wasn't in fact having a stroke, I figured that I either had a brain tumor or that I was just plain nuts. I lay there for a few more minutes and then it happened again. Only this time I could "see" in my mind these two very real, very strange-looking eyes. They looked like huge cat eyes, amber in color, with diamond-shaped pupils. I was so struck that I jumped about a foot off the bed! My husband was alarmed by my movement and he jumped up with me. He asked me if I was okay, so I told him what I had seen. He put his arm around me and eventually calmed down to a point where I thought I might be able to sleep again. As soon as I closed my eyes, again I saw the same "static" and heard that noise. But this time I could also hear people talking in a language that I didn't understand. I don't know how to explain what happened next, except to say that I could momentarily comprehend what was being said. I could hear a man, and he spoke these words: "prestigious listener in November."

It made absolutely no sense to me, and I jumped again at hearing it. I told my husband what I'd heard and I could see that he was really getting worried about me. "Maybe someone is trying to tell you something," said James. "You ought to write this all down." So, I went into the living room to grab a pencil and some paper. As I walked through the living room, I began to feel some kind of static electricity swirling all around me. Only, it didn't feel like regular static electricity. It started at my head and swirled right down to my toes. It was the strangest sensation. When I got back to the bedroom, I told James what I'd experienced in the living room and that I was feeling strange. I wrote what I remembered and then lay down next to my husband and tried to relax. As soon as I shut my eyes, I heard the man's voice again. This time, he spoke to me directly: "Are you still feeling strange?"

I nearly fell off the bed. Now my husband was *really* getting worried. I screamed at James, telling him what I'd just heard. "This is not funny!" I yelled. "Whatever is going on had better stop, now!" I lay down again, this time thinking to myself that I shouldn't close my eyes—every time I did, I could hear *him*! But I did close my eyes, and, sure enough, there he was again. "Ha, ha, ha, ha, ha," he laughed sarcastically. That did it. I was never going to go to sleep again because I would never be able to close my eyes without him invading my mind, whoever "he" was. Eventually, I grew so tired that sleep simply overpowered me—and apparently "him" too.

When I awoke the next day, I had the worst headache of my entire life. It felt like my head was about to explode. As a matter of fact, my whole body ached. I felt like I'd been hit by a train. This awful feeling lasted for three days before finally wearing off. I have not been the same since then. It was right after this episode that I began to have what I call "conversations with myself." I could be driving down the street, thinking about just any old thing, when suddenly these thoughts would come into my mind from who knows where. Words that made no sense to me would bug me to the point that I couldn't concentrate on what I was doing until I wrote them down. As soon as I would do so, they would go away and I could concentrate again. Much of what I "saw" and "heard" during these mental intrusions would become the basis of my drawings and of the notes I share later in this book.

On one occasion, while cutting the grass behind our house with our sit-on mower, I began to hear a little voice in my head talking about spiritual matters far beyond my understanding. I thought, "Okay, I'll bite. Tell me, what is God?" This is what I heard in response:

> God is the spirit of man. Look around you. All that is beautiful, all that is ugly with life is God. God is life. Unconditional Love is the highest manifestation of life, of God. There is but one life. Man is merely another manifestation of that life, which is God.

"Whoa! Okay," I thought, "this is getting out of hand here!"

One time, I asked about my baby—the baby I lost under mysterious circumstances in 1978. Where was she and why was she taken from me? This was the answer I received:

The child was necessary for your development, and ours. The greater good overrides all. The child is with us both. Her physical body is with us, but know this: the child's energy is uniquely yours. It is quite exciting, refreshing, hopeful. The child uses the name you chose for her. The child prefers it to our way. The child must remain with us for now. She has much to absorb. You cannot provide what is necessary with the exception of the human touch. We have not been able to simulate this yet. This will come from you. You have agreed to this. This child will then care for the needs of others. The human part of her is ever drawn to you. We do not fully understand this, nor can we prevent it. We will learn much from you and others like you. Know this, all is as it must be. All is right. These children are our hope for the future—your future and ours. Know that we mean no harm. We seek only to grow, to become as one, as all life must.

I couldn't begin to tell you where this came from. Perhaps my own mind was trying to justify the loss of my baby. Perhaps it came from some outside source we don't yet recognize. I have no idea for sure. But it meant something to me and I thought I would share it with you. Perhaps it will mean something to some of you reading this.

Some of what I remembered or "received" made little sense to me and I had no idea what I was supposed to do with it. I mean, who would I tell, and why would they even listen to me?

~

On September 29, 1993, I had a total hysterectomy. Everything happened so fast that I still find it hard to believe.

I had felt unwell for quite some time before I realized that my monthly periods were the cause. I had been concerned about my health ever since the night of my June 30, 1983 encounter (detailed in Chapter One). I'd witnessed first-hand the devastating effects of that encounter on our family dog, and I couldn't help but think that perhaps my own health may also have been compromised in a way that had yet to manifest. But how ever could I explain these fears to my new doctor? I had told him nothing of my experiences. I was afraid he'd think I was nuts.

I experienced physical pain for many years, complaining occasionally, but always chickening out when it was suggested I do something about it. I was afraid I had cancer, like my dog, and didn't want to know.

Eventually, the pain became too much to bear and I was forced to contact my doctor. It turned out that my concerns were justified. He told me I had a large tumor and that I needed a hysterectomy right away. I had suffered enough. As soon as I realized it was going to happen, I called Budd Hopkins. Budd didn't seem too surprised. He said I was probably one of the last remaining female abductees still to have all of her female parts intact, and that this happening to me was almost inevitable. He felt strongly that there was some connection between my current physical problems and my extraordinary experiences. If anything, that made me worry even more. Still, I appreciated his support and his encouraging words about how good I would feel after it was all over.

Six days before my surgery, on September 23, 1993, we had a terrific UFO sighting right out in front of our house. Four of us—myself, my fiancé K.O., and my friend Jeanne Robinson and her daughter, who were living with us at the time—saw and videotaped a tremendous, bright light as it hovered and skipped across the night sky just west of our farmhouse.

I had been sitting on the couch in the living room, watching television when a bright flashing light caught my eye through the front window of the house. I watched it for a moment. "It must be some kind of airplane," I told myself. But after around 30 seconds, I realized it was moving too erratically and was much too bright for an airplane. I jumped up from the couch and shouted, "Hey, you guys look at this!" K.O., Jeanne and her daughter all came running for the front door. After a few moments of "what the hell is that?" we all ran onto the front porch, tripping over each other to get a better look. I told K.O. to get the camcorder as the rest of us ran to the driveway. Seconds later, K.O. returned with the camcorder and we videotaped several minutes of the light as it grew brighter and then grew dim again. Soon, it appeared to drop just above tree level and move off into the distance.

We watched for several more minutes, until it was out of sight. Suddenly, I realized something was walking down the road toward me and my companions. I tried to reason that this must be some kind of wild animal. "A deer, that's what it is," I said to myself. When it reached the end of the fence, it stopped, cocked its head at me and began to walk backward! "Wait a minute! A deer can't walk backward. Besides, its legs and shoulders are moving funny, kind of gangly-looking. This was the strangest thing I had ever seen. It was too tall to be any kind of dog. I estimated its height to be about four feet. It was very thin and very pale in color. It was extremely dark out that night and I figured the only way we were able to see it was because it was reflecting what little moonlight there was. As a matter of fact, it almost looked as if it weren't quite all there at all, as if it were not fully materialized. Its head was light bulb shaped and its neck and shoulders were spindly. Its legs and arms were long and thin also. On the videotape you can hear Jeanne's daughter saying, "Momma, what's that in the road coming toward us?" Then, you can hear me scream. Suddenly, the mood changes and you can hear us talking excitedly about the light we had just seen. Nothing was ever said about the thing in the road again. By this time, K.O. had his little hand-held two-meter radio outside with us and you can hear an English fellow talking about how he could see colored fingers of light in the northern sky. He believed he was seeing the Northern Lights. The only things we could see when we looked north were clouds. Then you can hear K.O. talking about how he is recording some strange beeping sound that appeared to be coming from our cattle barn, north of the house. Later on in the tape, you can actually hear the beeping sound as K.O. takes the recorder closer to the barn. Then, we saw another light shoot behind us from the west, heading southeast. This light turned a deep, blood red before it shot out of sight. After we finally went back in the house and began to review what had just happened, we began to realize that there was some time missing—and several minutes of video, as well.

After we had seen the "animal" coming down the road toward us, but before K.O. began to record the beeping sound, I had recorded some of the sound myself. After we lost sight of the light for the last time, K.O. had gone in for a few minutes to call a friend of his who was on the other side of town. He wanted to have him look outside and see if he could see anything. Jeanne and I were outside alone at this point. This is when we first noticed the sounds.

Jeanne remembers the red light being on when I was taping and she also remembers how I marked each beep with a verbal confirmation. I even remember telling K.O. to turn the camcorder back on because I shut it off before he came back outside—and he remembered turning it back on before he went to the barn to record some more of the sound and to check on the cows. But my whole part of our tape is missing. Later, as we went back over the times and the tape, we realized we could only account for about eighteen-and-a-half minutes of a forty-five-minute episode. To this day, we still aren't sure what happened to the rest of the time—or to us.

~

When I went back to my surgeon for my six-week check-up after the surgery, I asked what exactly he had found. I reminded him that the doctor in Springfield who read my ultrasound scan told me I had a tumor in my uterus. I reminded him also that my own family doctor had felt what he thought was a rather large tumor in the same place. You can imagine my surprise, then, when my doctor told me he had found no tumor at all. Rather, he said I had something called adenomyosis, as well as cysts on both ovaries, scar tissue, adhesions and endometriosis. I definitely needed the hysterectomy, but I was tumor-free. Unusually, in the weeks and months following my surgery, I had no need for any estrogen supplements, even though I had a total hysterectomy. No symptoms of menopause, whatsoever. I still wonder what happened to whatever it was that the doctor saw on my ultrasound film. No one will ever know, yet I can't help but think it might have had something to do with the sighting we had just before I went in for the surgery. Under the circumstances, wouldn't you?

~

After all these years, the strange experiences have yet to stop. Time can pass quietly and I will think to myself, "Well, maybe it's over," and then, as if on cue, as if someone were listening, *weird* enters my life again. Fortunately, I have had witnesses to most of what I have had to deal with. Here are just a couple of more recent entries from my journal.

June 13, 2017

Bug buzzed my ear. I was sitting here on the couch talking to Dave when, all of a sudden, this huge buzzing sound, like a giant bee, buzzed in my ear. I could even feel as if someone was touching my ear and face! I literally jumped off the couch, flailing my arms around as if to swat whatever it was away. Dave was freaked. He says he saw or heard nothing and he was standing right in front of me! I made him look in my hair and ear (it was the right ear, the ear that "someone" stuck something in back on June 30, 1983). I got huge goose bumps all over and now I'm a bit freaked out. I keep looking around trying to see a bug. Ain't nothing in here. Damn.

November 1, 2018

I had a weird dream this morning and I think it was another test. This will be kind of long, sorry. Keep in mind I'm not religious. I prefer "spiritual." I don't call myself "Christian." I do not like what modern Christianity has become. I prefer to think of myself as a follower of the teachings of Christ. Having said that, right before I woke up this morning, I had a dream that a really scroungy, dirty, skinny tattooed man came to my door asking for incense. Tear drops and skeleton face literally tattooed on his face. And he was absolutely filthy. I answered him, "Yes, I have some that I will give you. Wait here." I went to my office to get the incense (it's a very expensive Indian incense). I had a flower in there that I picked up to give him, too. When I went back out to my living room, he was standing in my house. I said, "HEY! What the fuck are you doing in my house?" He said, "I can go anywhere I want" and laughed maniacally. I handed him the incense and flowers and said, "May God bless you and save your soul." He just stood there, staring at me, smirking, and slowly making the "jack off" motion with his fist. I thought, "I'm about to call Dave, and he will put the hurt on your ass" (Dave was in his back office). I said to the guy, "Get out of my house, right now! And may God save your soul." He turned and left, looking over his shoulder at me as he did. At that point, I woke up. I got out of bed and went into the living room. Dave was sitting in there. He immediately proceeded to tell me there had been a white van parked in our driveway for about fifteen minutes and he left right before I came out of the bedroom. He said he was about to call the police. Dave was extremely agitated; it made him feel "creepy." I felt that the van had something to do with this extremely vivid, realistic dream. I know how crazy that sounds, believe me! I feel like I was just tested. Just another weird day in my weird life.

SEVEN

Questions and Answers

~

In October of 1988, I was invited to attend a retreat and to sit on an abduction panel in Aspen, Colorado. The idea was to invite a number of scientists and other experts to this beautiful location to hear what the abductees had to say about their encounters. They were going to put their heads together in an effort to come up with some answers (though in reality I'm sure we only came up with more questions).

It was a fascinating trip and I was glad I made the journey, despite my not faring too well in the high altitude. I had an opportunity to meet some of the most important individuals in the field, including Travis Walton, Betty Hill and Charles Hickson, to name a few. I had the opportunity to talk with them face-to-face and to hear their stories direct from their own mouths—to "feel" their emotions as they talked. It was a powerful experience.

One of the most important people I was to meet in Aspen turned out not to be an experiencer, but a researcher by the name John Carpenter. He would ultimately help me to better understand myself and to regain control of my life, and I will be forever grateful to God for bringing us together.

I'll never forget the evening I spent in John's suite with him and his wife, Denise, spilling my guts about all the strange things that I had been remembering and documenting over the years. At first, I was a little embarrassed about what I was telling him, fully aware that what I was saying sounded crazy. But I figured what the heck—he was a shrink. If anyone could tell me whether I was losing my mind, he could. I think I wanted him to tell me just that. At least mental illness is treatable. Instead, he excitedly began telling me about all these other people he had been working with recently who had been having similar experiences to mine for years. A part of me thought, "oh, shit!" But another part of me was wild with relief and excitement. This might really mean something!

I have no idea why I zeroed in on John earlier that evening, or why I felt that I had to share my memories with him. I couldn't decide if I was remembering information that someone had told me long ago during my experiences, or if I was receiving some kind of communication in the present. A lot of my memories of the phenomenon feel so much a part of me that I can't help but feel as if I were born with them—that they are embedded in my soul. For some reason, these kinds of coincidences—synchronicities, if you will—happen frequently in relation to extraordinary experiences. I think we were destined to meet.

As we sat there talking, I could sense a growing mutual excitement. I definitely got the feeling that speaking to John was the right thing to do.

As I began to share with John my memories and, let's call them "downloads," I could barely believe his response. He was reciting my own words back to me, almost verbatim. I had not told anyone, including Budd, about some of the things I had begun to recall. "Where in the hell did he hear this! How did he know?" I thought. This is not the kind of stuff that comes up in everyday conversation. Hell, I was still trying to figure out if I had lost my mind!

John told me about a woman he was working with, named Jeanne. He thought we should meet. As soon as I heard him say those words, I jumped. I knew that was why I was there. I had to meet this woman. John began to share with me some of the details Jeanne had been writing down for him. I was stunned that many of her words were almost identical to mine.

I learned that she was as mystified about some of her writings as I was about mine, and she, too, had grave concerns about her mental health. I knew for a fact that I had never met this woman, nor had we ever communicated with one another on the phone or by mail. It just blew me away that we were writing about the same things. I think John was pretty flipped out by it, too.

Before we left Aspen, we exchanged addresses and phone numbers. I thanked Denise for her patience and for allowing me to keep her and John up so late that night, and John gave me Jeanne's address.

I couldn't wait to get home and to write to Jeanne. As my pen flowed over the pages of that first letter, I couldn't help but notice how the hand that held it was trembling. I felt breathless as page after page of memories poured out of me. I was keen to cite to Jeanne the correlations that John had pointed out to me when we had talked that night in Aspen. Oh, how I wished that Jeanne had been in Aspen! This would have been so much easier, face-to-face. My hand could barely keep pace with my mind, and my writing began to deteriorate rapidly. Finally, I had to call it a night. I finished my letter the following morning.

On October 26, 1988, I received a letter from Jeanne. John had given her my address and had told her about our similarities. Apparently, she had written her letter to me the same day I had written mine to her—and her letter to me reached me first! Hers—more than half a dozen pages—contained almost the same details as mine. It was like reading my own letter back to myself. Here's just a little of what she wrote, and I quote it with her permission:

> First of all, I want to thank you for putting your experiences in book form. It was your book [actually, Budd Hopkins' book], *Intruders*, and the article in *OMNI Magazine*, which began to stir up my memories... I really thought I was a nutcase during those two years. I used to bitch myself out for even considering the possibility of it all. Uncovering all this stuff has been a relief and a headache. I've gone through stages of terrible aloneness and feeling different from everyone I know. Here I was, remembering all these amazing, incredible things and I had no one to talk to about it. While reading *Intruders*, I was relating to your experiences and not knowing why. There was a familiarity to it that frightened me. I knew, even back then, that I really wanted to talk to you. Now, I have the chance. Everything John told me really blew me away! Damn, woman, we've obviously seen the same things! All of this really hasn't sunk in. But it's more verification, and that's what I need. I still have trouble believing it all.

I can't describe to you how it felt to hear from someone who could really understand what I was feeling. As I read her letter, I felt like crying with relief. She really understood! She knew! I won't share the full letter here because it could take up a whole chapter of its own. But, I will tell you that the details we compared were nearly identical, along with how we felt about it all.

Jeanne and I are still very close. As a matter of fact, we eventually lived together in the same house for a while in 1993—Jeanne, her daughter, my two sons and my new husband, K.O.—one big happy family. When Jeanne and her daughter pulled up in my driveway, I felt the relief one feels when all the kids are finally home, just as the big storm is about to hit. Even though she is a few years older than me, I feel very protective of her. She feels like my child.

Jeanne and I would later participate in a test of sorts, for John Carpenter and a man named Forest Crawford. Forest was a friend of John's and he was also a state section director for the MUFON group in Illinois. They had devised a test for abductees who were remembering/ receiving information. They were looking for correlations in the information. Boy, did they find it in Jeanne and me! With the blessing of Forest and Jeanne, I will share with you, here, some of the correlating information gleaned from Jeanne and myself:

Questions to the UFO intelligences

How do you use light?

> **Debbie:** "Light, in its many forms, can be used in many different ways: nutrition, healing tissue, travel, disassemble molecules/pass through (as) light/reassemble, light as a means of self-propulsion."

> **Jeanne:** "We travel by means of light fusion. We are able to travel great distances using this power. It is a transformation of light energy to light fuel. It is efficient and powerful. We have harnessed this energy and magnified it to transport us in our travels through the universe. You were brought onboard our craft by means of spectral transport. Your essence was blended with the light beam. It is one method of matter transference. The light particles penetrate your atomic structure, which is recorded into the transponder memory. Matter is then reconstructed at the desired site of appearance. Light penetration of matter causes matter to become light, which can be controlled and directed to the chosen area of reintegration."

What is the purpose of the implants?

Debbie: "Tracking, monitoring of the individual and sensory receptors, and occasionally altering the energy level of the individual to facilitate necessary communications and molecular changes for the greater good, through adjustment of energy levels."

Jeanne: "The sensory implants have many uses. They are tracking devices. They record sensory input from the subjects. They register pollution levels in the subject. They measure stress levels. We are able to study migration habits of your people. It enables us to communicate with our test-subjects, even from great distances. It is a constant surveillance for our chosen ones. The implants are also warning devices capable of alerting us to certain dangers threatening the individual. It lessens the possibility of premature death of the chosen. They cannot be completely protected but it minimizes our loss."

Do you eat or drink?

Debbie: "Absorption through the outer covering of the body, skin, through the soft tissue inside the mouth. Energy ray, (light of some kind?) nutritional fluids. Waste excreted through the skin. We do not drink as you understand drink. Do not 'swallow;' fluid is absorbed through the tissue in the mouth."

Jeanne: "Our method of consumption is very different from your own. We absorb what we need from our environment and yours. It is similar to photosynthesis. We need light, mineral substances not existing on your planet, proteins and moisture."

What is God?

Debbie: "There is no perfect religion, no perfect people. There is only life. Life, in its purest form is the beginning, the base from which all that exists originated. Yours, mine, all life, are merely tributaries of a great river. We hold all life in highest esteem, for we are all a part of that life. This is not blind faith. We swam 'the river,' so to speak, and you too shall swim 'the river' when you are fully prepared. These words to which you restrict yourself make it very difficult to pass on to you the information you seek. Religion is a sociological phenomenon, unique to your species. This is a creation of the human. Not to be confused with the 'Spirit.' What you call 'God' is 'Spirit.' Jesus was a man, created by 'Spirit' to help you to understand, on your own level, in your own terms and times. Obviously, you were not ready. The process will continue until you have reached the level of understanding set forth for your form of life by 'Spirit' from which you have come. Can you possibly understand? You have made your lives of choice, of free will and you have left no room for 'Spirit' within you. Now is the time to begin to remember that from which you came. Look into yourself. Look about you. All that is beautiful, all that is ugly, but with soul, all that radiates life, is 'Spirit,' is what you call 'God.' You are blind, distracted by your lives. You have let negativity and fear keep the inner eye closed. Do not fear. 'God' is life, eternal. Our greater good is that which works together to bring to 'Spirit', that to which it belongs. To give IT strength and life. For to bring IT life, we give life to ourselves. Remember, there is only life if you believe, there is only love if you believe, there is only evil if you believe. If you believe that these things exist for you then, they will. If you do not believe that they exist for you then, they will not. You have been given this choice. You create your own reality. You are the Creator."

Jeanne: "As I have told you before, God is the life essence of the Universe. We relate to this essence through respect for all life. We protect life when it is endangered. This is our goal. Our method of worship is a meditation to our inner selves. We become attuned to the universal life-force."

Some people have suggested that we were channeling this information. I really don't know. I am not sure what to think about channeling. I can't help but feel that a lot of this has always been with me. Or, at least, that someone "taught" me all this information years ago, when I was just a little kid, and it's been locked up in my subconscious, waiting for the right time—for me to "wake up" and remember.

I would start to remember/receive information at the strangest times. I would be doing anything from washing dishes to driving my son to baseball practice, when something would come to me. Strange thoughts would invade my mind to the point where I could no longer concentrate on what I was doing until I wrote down whatever it was I was remembering/receiving. I have even had to pull my car to the side of the road and write something down because I was afraid I would have an accident if I didn't. It always seemed to hit me like a ton of bricks. I would be so exhausted afterward that I would often take a little nap, whenever possible.

More than once, I awakened from deep sleep state with whole paragraphs floating around in my head, and there was no way I would be able to get back to sleep until I wrote it all down. I wrote several poems this way, but it would be years before I fully understood their deeper meaning. Some of the technical information that came to me was way beyond my knowledge base. The anxiety I felt before something would come to me was terrific. I would sweat and tremble. I felt the weight of information might make my head burst! But eventually it would rise to the surface of my consciousness. I'd write it down, and immediately the pressure would ease, until it built up for the next time.

I did several of the drawings in this book in the same manner. I was able to look at a blank piece of paper and "see"—on the paper—what I had to draw. It was as if something in my mind was projecting the image onto the blank sheet, and I just traced the images and filled in the shadows.

In 1989, someone came into my home while I was out of town and took two art pads full of sketches, two journals and the sculpture of an alien head I had crafted years before. They also read my diary. Whoever it was left our back door wide open and left other tell-tale signs of their presence. They neglected to touch our expensive video and game equipment, or anything else in the house that was of value. They may have taken my physical property, but they can never remove what's in my head. Everything is burned so deeply into my mind that I will never forget any of it.

"They" had told me that sleep would bring answers. I was told that anxiety slowed the process and that sleep was optimum for remembering. So, when John gave me the set of questions to answer, I took "their" advice. Every night, before I went to sleep, I read one of John's questions to myself. It would be the last thing I would have in my conscious mind before drifting off. First thing in the morning, I would read the question again, and write down the first thing that came to me. This is how I finally remembered most of what I wrote. Here are a few more examples of what I remembered—or was told:

Question: *Why not a face-to-face confrontation with humans?*

Answer: "You are physically much stronger than us. To stand face-to-face with many of you would be foolish and dangerous. Also, for many of you—the mind could not accept all that we are. To physically touch us would be dangerous for you. The mind is not equipped. 'Blow a fuse?' Understand? You and others like you are re-structured, have the capability to absorb without danger. We radiate many things, unintentional. It is our way of "knowing" one another. Also, we radiate energy that is harmful to many human functions and tissue. To avoid physical contact is primarily for your (humans') safety."

Question: *How do we cure schizophrenia?*

Answer: "Thought dysfunction; study the DNA—changes in the structure are observed with this dysfunction. Why do you continually ask for information on repairing yourselves? You have this knowledge already; why do you not use it for the benefit of all? This is wasteful" (its tone of voice sounded as if it was pretty annoyed with me! I didn't expect that!).

Question: *How do you travel in your ships?*

Answer: "Once here, we utilize the electromagnetic waves of your planet [in my mind, I could see the waves of the ocean and visualized the leaf of a tree floating and drifting, riding the waves, back and forth. Don't ask me why!]. We have ships built solely for use on this planet. Other, larger ships that travel much farther, utilize different means of propulsion, depending on distance traveled. Pass through glitches in the continuum by bending light and time (your words)."

This is probably the creepiest thing they ever told me: "Don't force memory. When we are ready, you will remember. Anxiety slows our process. Hypnosis will not reveal what is encoded into your genetic structure. Proper body chemistry will. You are currently resistive. This is understood and was expected. We have begun acceleration. Know this: all is as it must be."

Please remember, as you read these pages, I am only telling you what I've remembered. I'm not sure what it all means or if it even means anything at all. Somehow, I get the feeling that what we are remembering is not as important as the fact that we *are* remembering. I think *that* means something. This whole process is not quite the same as "hearing voices." It's thoughts and ideas, visual images that often times I must use my own words to describe. This can be tough when your vocabulary is limited to begin with. It was a relief to finally meet someone who was having the same thing happening to her and to find out that we weren't alone. There are hundreds, perhaps thousands of people just like Jeanne and I. Perhaps even your neighbor or your siblings are like us. It's not surprising that most people will never talk about this openly and I realize that I took a chance when I decided to. Somebody had to do it.

~

John and Forest made arrangements for Jeanne and me to meet in St. Louis, Missouri. I really couldn't wait to meet her and I was looking forward to the event with great anticipation.

Finally, on April 18, 1990, Jeanne and I met—face-to-face—for the first time. When I looked into her eyes, I knew. I could see in her what I felt in myself. I knew that there was one hell of a lot more to this whole UFO/abduction thing than anyone could ever have dreamed. I knew that it went way beyond genetic manipulation or anything else researchers had begun to conclude. I'm not saying they are all wrong, by any means. I had just come to realize that no one had it all wrapped up. What John and Forest were doing was of the utmost importance, not just for Jeanne and me, but also for all human beings. I'm telling you that Jeanne, myself, and people like us are living proof that something much bigger is happening and it is time for us to open our eyes and see the bigger picture. Start listening and really hear. Start talking and be truthful, not embarrassed by what you remember. Don't ridicule what you don't understand because it may just happen to you next.

I had purchased a small crystal pyramid at a gift shop in town, several months before I started writing to Jeanne. Whenever I received a letter from her, I would use that pyramid as a paperweight to hold the pages down as I read. (I did a lot of reading on the front porch at my old house. The light was good and the breeze was relaxing). I had thought about sending it to Jeanne because we had several conversations about pyramid shapes and the significance they held for us. When I realized that we would be meeting in St. Louis, I held off sending it so that I could give it to her in person when we met. I thought it would be a nice token of our friendship.

When I got to the hotel room, Jeanne was there. We were to be roommates. Cool! As I started to unpack my bags, I came across the pyramid I had packed for Jeanne. When I took it out and gave it to her, I thought she was going to cry. Her jaw dropped and I heard her gasp as she plopped down on the bed. After she regained her composure, she told me that she had been drawing the exact three-dimensional shape, almost obsessively, for the past week. She said that somehow she knew she needed to have one. She had been looking all over her town, trying to find one that she could buy. I told her that I thought I would give it to her as a token of friendship and that I felt it would help her focus her thoughts. I felt that she needed to have it.

The whole time we were together, we were virtually inseparable. We also realized that we could practically read each other's minds. When we thought something, the other thought it, too. It was the most incredible feeling I have ever had. Meeting Jeanne awakened something inside me. The bond that we developed was far-and-away greater than any bond two people could expect to share. It seemed deeper even than the bond shared by people who have experienced similar traumas. It was as if we were one entity. We are like sisters, to this day.

~

Unfortunately, I still had a long way to go, as far as getting a grip on my fear was concerned. I wasn't quite as strong as I thought I was, even after meeting Jeanne. That old saying about strength in numbers isn't always true.

On July 25, 1990, I was sitting in front of my open kitchen window, talking on the phone to John Carpenter. Earlier, my oldest son had come into the kitchen to tell me that his nose had started bleeding and that he couldn't get it to stop. I got him taken care of and resumed my conversation. After John and I hung up, I decided to go back to my son's bedroom and check on him before I turned in for the night. It was getting pretty late. Right before I stood up from my chair, I saw several bright flashes in the kitchen. Then there seemed to be some kind of power surge, which caused the lights to get very bright. Then they grew dimmer than they should have been. I went into my bedroom to wake my husband to ask him if there might be a problem with the air conditioner—perhaps that was the cause. He was of little help in his groggy state.

I decided to go to the bathroom before I hit the sack, and it was a good thing I did... As I came out of the bathroom and turned towards my son's room to check on him, I was confronted by the sight a small grey entity, standing at the end of the hallway. I jumped about a foot off the ground and screamed louder that I thought I ever could. From the feeling I got as I looked at his face, I think I surprised him as well. I got the distinct impression that I wasn't supposed to have seen him. That didn't stop me from tearing off down the hall, sliding around the doorway into my bedroom, and slapping at the light switch with my open hand. The lights came on and then went off again as I dove from the doorway into the bed. (If you could see the layout of my bedroom, you'd know what a feat this was!). Needless to say, my husband was now wide awake.

I buried my face in the pillow next to him and clung on to him for dear life. He kept shaking me and screaming, "What's wrong, Debbie? What did you see? What's out there?" But I couldn't speak. I guess I was in shock. I could hear him yelling at me but I just could not respond.

It took all of ten minutes before I could actually talk to my husband and tell him what I had seen. When I finally lifted my head to look at him, I could see that the pillow I had been clutching was stained with blood. Not a huge amount, but enough to see that there was something wrong. Then I noticed two triangular-shaped gouges in the palm of my left hand. They were bleeding rather profusely. At first, I first thought I had cut myself on the light-switch plate I'd slapped as I sailed around the door and onto the bed. But no, when I finally got up and looked at the switch plate, there was no blood to be seen, and nothing sharp there on which to have cut myself. I still don't know how it happened. Would you believe, throughout all this commotion, my son never woke up? The next day he was fine and had no recollection of the night before, including his crazy mother's screams. Lucky kid!

The mark in my parents' back yard, pictured in August, 1983.

Winter of 1983. Snow melting off the mark and strip.
It did this all winter.

The mark in my parents' yard, pictured approximately
one year after the event.

My dog, Penny Lane. She was out in the back yard before me on the
night of June 30, 1983. Soon thereafter her health began to fail. She
is pictured here as her fur was beginning to fall out and sores were
developing on her back. Before long, she was losing fur all over her
body, and her teeth fell out.

The front door to Budd's apartment/studio in New York City. It was a place that represented hope for me. Eventually, it came to feel like home. The building, which was an important part of my life, is now gone.

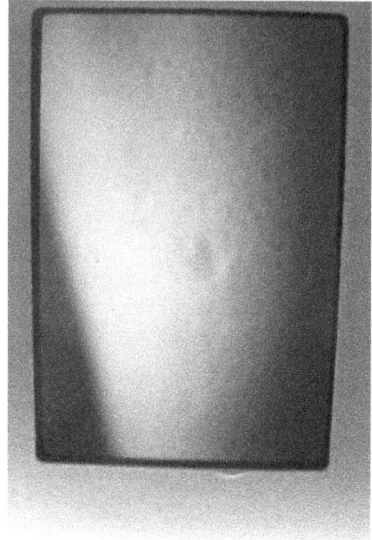

The scoop mark on my right shin. My mother has one identical to mine and in the same place.

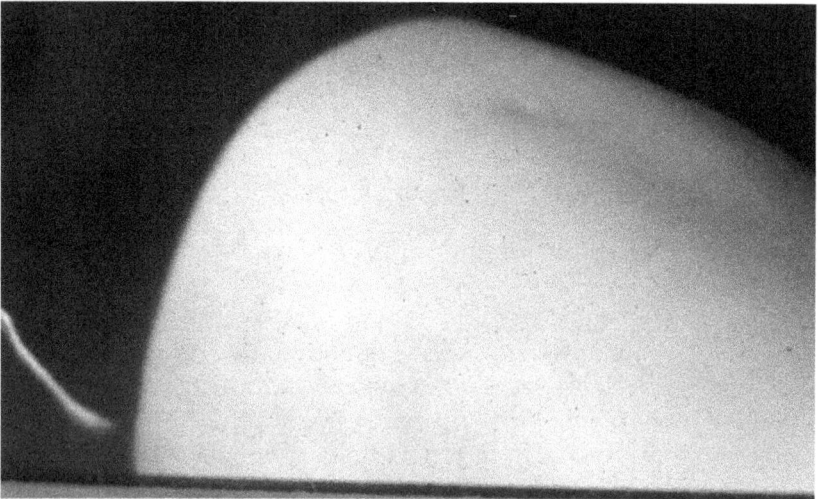

My mother's scoop mark on her shin.

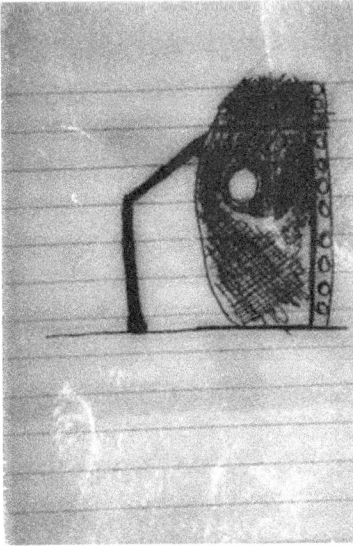

My original sketch for Budd of the "craft" I saw in my parents' back yard on June 30, 1983.

The gray guy I remembered seeing in my room in 1978. He was one of two. I would see him/her/it a few more times along the way over the ensuing years.

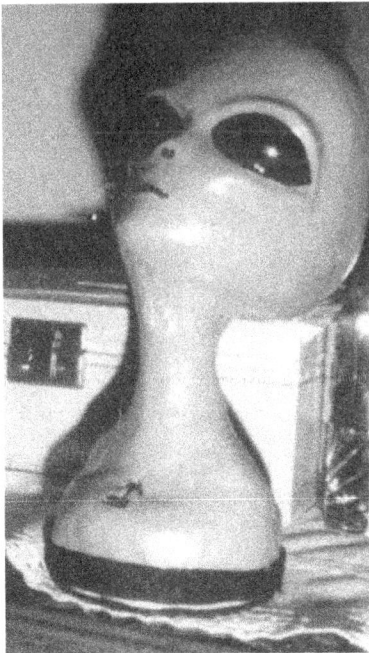

A sculpture I made for Budd. I felt strongly that I wanted something in 3D, like I could see it in my mind when I remembered it. Eventually someone came into my home and took it. We never found the culprit and we never saw the sculpture again.

The April 1984 experience that I shared with my mother. This was the drawing I did for Dr. Hynek.

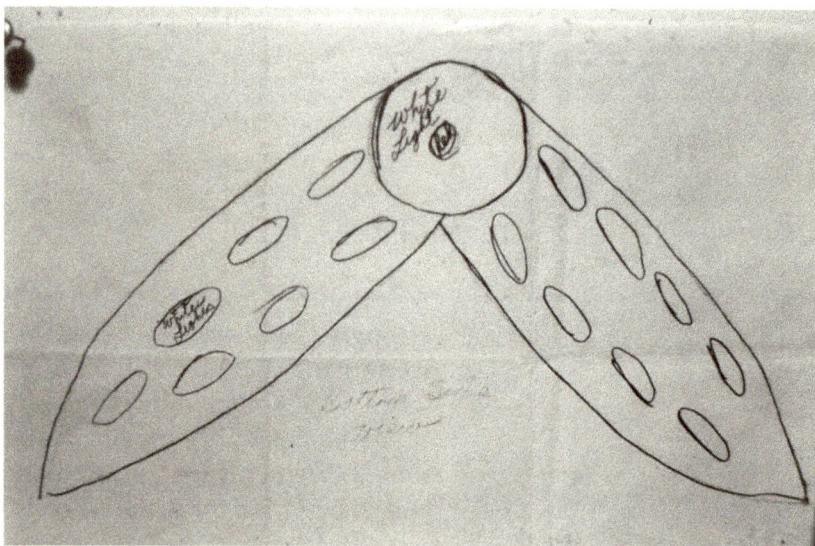

My mother's drawing for Dr. Hynek of our shared experience of April 1984.

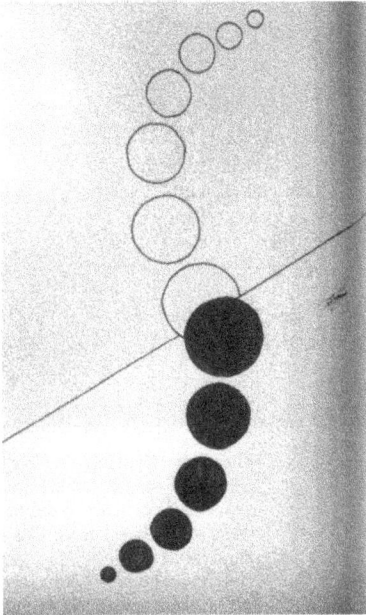

I drew this after a dream in which I saw this pattern. 1991.

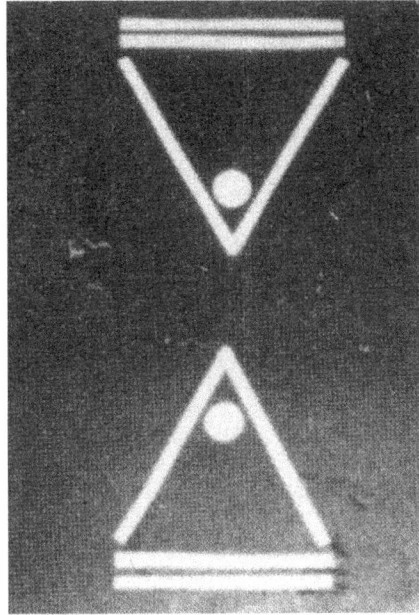

One of my early cardboard cut-outs of something I remembered seeing when I was in a place other than my home, possibly on a ship of some kind. I am not sure where I was. The walls were black and shiny, like polished stone. These markings were engraved into it.

Another cardboard cut-out that I made of various symbols I recalled seeing in the place with black walls. The writing was engraved. I felt that some of the symbols represented numbers, or perhaps a date.

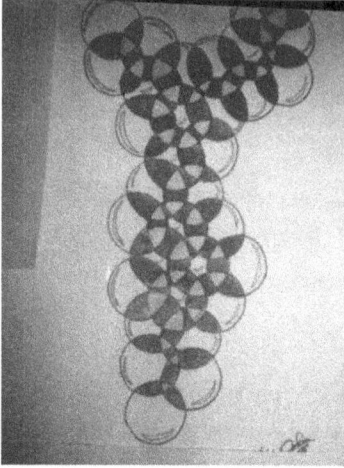

I called this "Casey's bubbles." I saw this image in a lucid dream and I think it was used as a tool to show me something. Each "bubble" represents a distinct universe.

In those small areas where the universes touch, contact is possible. But the contact areas are constantly shifting. The whole thing undulates, almost as if it were alive.

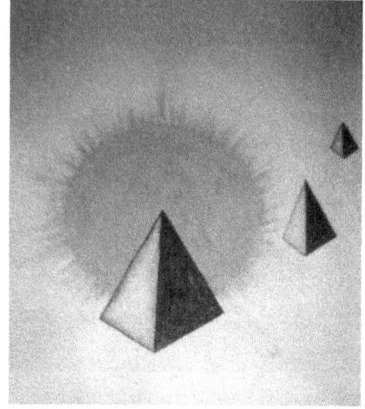

A symbol I dreamt about. In the dream I was told that this represented me (humans). This is how I was identified.

I saw this in a vivid dream. I drew it immediately upon waking.

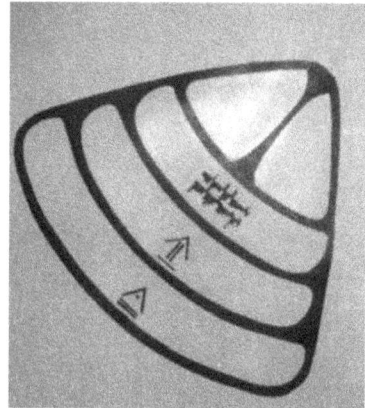

Symbols within a symbol. The one in the top section represented sound or music.

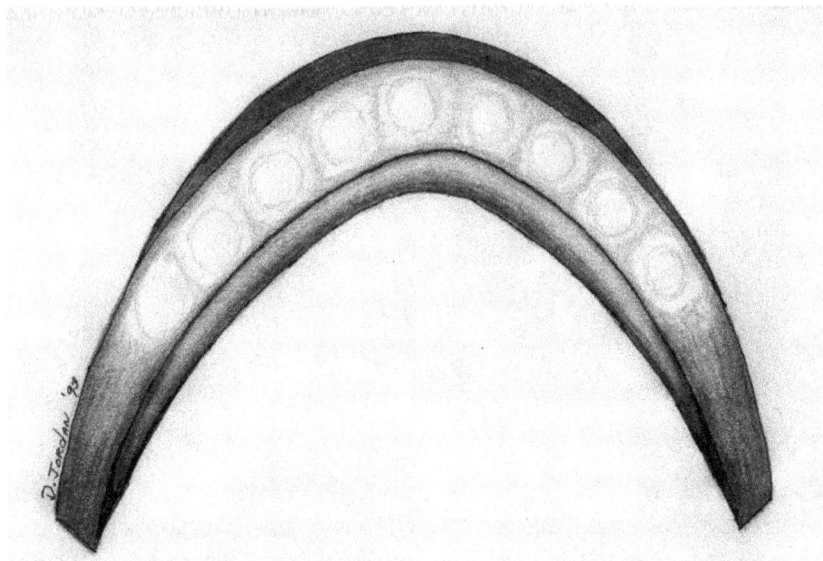

I awoke one morning in 1993 from a very vague dream and this image was stuck in my head. It wouldn't let me alone until I drew it, as was often the case.

An example of how close some of these black helicopters would get to us. This was a rare one because it actually had numbers on it. Most of them had no markings whatsoever.

A young, freaked-out me (on the left) in Aspen Colorado with Betty Hill, Travis Walton and Rosemary Osnato

Calvin Parker, myself and Budd Hopkins in Daytona Beach, 1991.

Budd and I in Connecticut at the Omega Conference, circa 1988.

Myself and my dear friend, Peter Robbins.

Tracy Torme, myself and Travis Walton being interviewed by John Ilias in California.

Budd and I in Pensacola, Florida, 1993.

Linda Mouton Howe, James Clarkson, Travis Walton, Kathleen Marden and I in Eureka Springs, Arkansas, April 2017.

My friend and co-host Gregg Cable and myself doing our Midwest Paratalk podcast from a remote location.

CMT's Katie Cook, Yvonne Smith and myself at the International UFO Congress Conference, Arizona, 2018.

This is a drawing I did after waking up from a dream in which this creature, which I called "the old sad woman," was peaking at me from an open doorway. Late-1980s.

This was my attempt to draw a picture of the
female child I saw during the "presentation" scene.
Her hair was actually wispy and white.

AMERICAN
mensa
LTD.

A NOT-FOR-PROFIT CORPORATION OF NEW YORK STATE • 2626 E. 14th ST., BROOKLYN, NY 11235-3992 Tel. (718) 934-3700 FAX: (718) 332-1183

03/26/93

DEBBIE JORDAN
1255 S KITLEY AV
INDIANAPOLIS IN 46203

DEAR DEBBIE JORDAN:

CONGRATULATIONS!

WE HAVE SCORED YOUR SUPERVISED TESTS WITH THE FOLLOWING
RESULTS:

CTMM	I.Q. 135	PERCENTILE 99
CATTELL B	I.Q. 141	PERCENTILE 95

SINCE YOU HAVE MET MENSA'S ADMISSION REQUIREMENT OF A TEST
SCORE AT OR ABOVE THE 98TH PERCENTILE, WE ARE HAPPY TO OFFER
YOU MEMBERSHIP IN THE SOCIETY.

AS SOON AS WE RECEIVE YOUR MEMBERSHIP DUES, WE SHALL ADD YOUR
NAME TO THE MEMBERSHIP ROSTER. A MEMBERSHIP CARD WILL BE SENT
TO YOU SHORTLY THEREAFTER, AND A LITTLE WHILE LATER YOU WILL
BEGIN TO RECEIVE THE NATIONAL AND LOCAL PUBLICATIONS.

IN THE MEANTIME, YOU MAY WANT TO BEGIN PARTICIPATING IN SOME
OF THE ACTIVITIES OF YOUR LOCAL GROUP. TO DO SO, WE SUGGEST
THAT YOU CONTACT YOUR LOCAL SECRETARY, WHOSE NAME, ADDRESS,
AND TELEPHONE NUMBER ARE LISTED BELOW.

WE HOPE THAT YOU WILL FIND YOUR MEMBERSHIP IN MENSA BOTH
ENJOYABLE AND SATISFYING.

SINCERELY,

S/SHARON BETTINGER
TESTING AND ADMISSIONS DEPT

LOCAL SECRETARY, GROUP # 461

        RICHARD J BARBRICK
        624 N DEARBORN ST
        INDIANAPOLIS IN 46201-2416

TELEPHONE # (317) 632-4747

The invitation I received from American MENSA showing my
IQ test scores.

12/13/77 vag. discharge, monilial. Rx Monostat cream

2/23/78 problem with catching and clicking with the R T-M joint. X-ray ordered preg test done which tends to be pos. X-RAY CANCELED

3/2/78 Preg test - neg

3/13/78 in for preg test which was neg, two wks ago it was pos. Will ordered another one at the hosp, most likely she is

5/5/78 in with cramping in the morn and after intercourse at nite. Has tenderness in the uterus. Has mild infection. Started on Vibramycin and Bentyl 20mgs

5/8/78 Rx Doxinatal, Mylanta & Cl. tips. Stop Bentyl.

5/9/78 diarrhea o Her colitis is acting up. Rx ProBanthine and if no imp, will use Lomotil

9/19/78 having abd cramping , pain, colitis. No rel. with ProBanthine before, just gradually got better on diet. Will try Bentyl 20mgs

0 10/2/78 pneumonia; seen at the hosp . Still coughing immensley. Placed on urgent list for adm. to CHI. Cont on Keflex given to her at hosp. then will switch to KIE in the meantime

10-17-79 2d. Home

10/2/78 still having cough and no temp; productive of white sputum. Sent lab for cult. chest x-ray and legioniers titer. Given Rx Minocin 50mgs q.i.d. and Quadrinol

11/29/78 Urine neg Preg test neg B/P140/82

12/5/78 Preg test pos Referred to Dr. McCree

7/31/79 B/P140/90

7/31/79 UTI; Rx Bactrim one b.i.d.

8/2/79 in for reaction to Bactrim; is having a rash and swelling. Rx Tetracycline today 500mgs q.i.d. Will d.c. Bactrim. Given Lasix for swelling.

9/10/79 /20/80

9/10/79 in for h.a. and B/P doing well. Started on Micrainum as needed for h.a.

11/13/79 R Slow K 2 b/d

12-11-79 Lamotil tabs

12/18/79 Is having problems with "flip-flopping of her heart". I can't tell whether it's a tachycardia or just palpitations. Was ck'd by Dr. Decatur last night and was given an unknown injection which knocked her out. Exam today is normal. Rx Valium 2mg t.i.d. Advised to count her pulse when this occurs and to report back if medication doesn't help.

Chart notes from my physician showing the date of the visit during I learned that I was pregnant—a pregnancy that would end tragically and mysteriously. This was how most family doctors charted office visits back in the days before laptops and intranet.

EIGHT

Acceleration

~

One aspect of this phenomenon that never ceases to amaze me is the profound and undeniable changes that we go through during and after our experiences. I call it "waking up." This seems to take longer for some of us than for others, yet we all seem to be moving in the same direction. Those of us who survive relatively intact seem to be evolving into an entirely new being. We have one foot in the linear mode of thinking—that which exists only in our minds— and one foot in the higher plane of free thought. It is almost as if, during an experience, we are reborn, ready to grow into a new and improved model. Our priorities change, and what used to be important to us— the things we used to worry about—no longer matter in the broader scheme of life.

We seem also to develop the ability to sense this same shift within others, to the point that we feel drawn to one another, like moths to a flame. The power of that attraction is so great that even geographical distance means nothing to us. We overcome tremendous obstacles just to be together. And when we are together, we quietly draw strength from one another. I believe this goes far beyond the sharing of a traumatic event, although I am certain that is a small part of it. When we find one another, it is as if we have found a little piece of ourselves—our heart and soul. We share an unspoken and often unconscious knowledge that no words can describe. We feel certain emotions that the confinement of human speech and written words prevent us from expressing fully. We love so deeply, so unconditionally, that it is overwhelming to those who have not yet discovered that part of themselves. We all seem to share an intense desire to help others feel this way, for themselves, for those around them, for this planet, and for all life.

I have spent years contemplating these matters and, after discussing it with family, friends, and with those whom I consider to be my teachers and mentors, I have reached the conclusion that I was born into this life with a purpose. As the years pass, and as I mature, this purpose has become clearer to me. I have learned that the most important thing I can do with the insight gleaned from my experiences is to concentrate on how I fit into the bigger picture, and do the best I can with what I have to benefit humanity and myself. I have realized that I cannot always control the situations in which I find myself, but I *can* control how I choose to react to those situations, emotionally and spiritually. I am certain that I am not the only one to finally remember what we are all supposed to be doing. I believe there are hundreds-of-thousands of us just now beginning to "wake up."

I began talking to several researchers who were beginning to realize the same things and who wondered what it all meant. They had, in recent years, begun receiving material that echoed much of what I had been communicating to them. One of these researchers was Linda Moulton Howe, an Emmy-Award-winning television documentary producer, radio personality and author. We became close so quickly that I suspect she is more involved in this whole thing than she thinks she is. But I won't go into that here. I think many of the researchers in the field of UFOs are more deeply connected than they know. Even the debunkers are "driven" to debunk for a reason (and some of them are so "driven" that they are about to drive over the edge!). Love, hate and fear are emotions of passion. In order for one to have great passion about something, there has to be some kind of emotional investment in the subject. If the loudest, most obnoxious debunkers didn't have a very deep emotional investment in the subject of UFOs, then they just simply wouldn't care what other people thought or believed. They wouldn't take it upon themselves to "set the world straight."

Whenever something unusual happened, I would call Linda. It was more like talking to a friend than talking to a researcher. She would document what I told her, for future reference, just in case. In January of 1992, I called Linda. I had awakened in a frenzy, very excited and "up." I just knew that something wonderful was about to happen. I told Linda that I felt as if this was the year my life would change. That *everything* about me and my life would change and it would be wonderful! I have awakened in good moods before, but this was ridiculous! I had never felt like this and immediately I thought to call Linda and tell her how I felt. Sure enough, in the months that followed, wild things began to happen.

In March of 1992, I won $1,000.00 on a radio contest. I had never won anything like this in my entire life. I also met a really neat person that month. His name was Joe. He'd been having a difficult time dealing with experiences similar to mine, and one of his close friends had contacted Indiana MUFON, looking for some help for him. Jerry Seivers, Indiana MUFON assistant state director, contacted me with Joe's address. We exchanged letters and soon made plans to meet.

We agreed to meet at the Denny's restaurant, close to my home. I got there around fifteen minutes before Joe. My husband James and I ordered coffee and waited for Joe to arrive. Joe told me he would be wearing a sweatshirt with a wolf printed on it. Several men entered the restaurant wearing sweatshirts and I looked them over, wondering if they were Joe. They weren't. When he did come in, he was wearing a jacket. I guessed he must have forgotten he'd told me to look for the sweatshirt. But, for some reason, I knew who he was. I just happened to be looking at the door when he came in, and I jumped a foot! I turned to James and said, "That's him! I know it!" James was rather shocked at my reaction but, having lived in my weird world for some time now, he just sat back and watched the whole thing unfold.

Joe turned in my direction, made eye contact with me, and let go with the biggest grin I have ever seen. It was instant recognition; instant friendship.

The three of us sat in the restaurant together for at least two hours, talking over coffee. It was an eye-opening experience. Joe and I found that we shared a great many memories and thoughts. It was the strangest feeling, talking to Joe, as if he and I were sharing the same mind. I got the distinct impression that we had done this before, at another time, in another life, if that's possible. I felt very protective of him, just as I had felt about Jeanne.

As we said our goodbyes in the parking lot, Joe handed me a book he had read that he wanted me to read. The book was called, *Black Elk Speaks*. Joe knew, through our letters, that I had become interested in Native American heritage since I discovered I have Native American ancestry. He felt I would find the book interesting, and he was right. He also told me of another book he felt I should read. It was titled, *Return of the Bird Tribes*, by Ken Carey. He'd lend it to me at our next meeting two weeks later at my house.

During that next meeting with Joe, I was amazed at how my animals reacted to him. They were all over him and seemed to sense he was a good person—a truly special person. My birds sang for him and my dog and cat wouldn't leave him alone, each wanting to sit on his lap. My animals had never reacted to a stranger like this before. I was quite surprised!

We sat up talking late into the night. Even James seemed to be mesmerized by Joe's soft voice and gentle manner. Before Joe left that night, he handed me the book he had brought with him and I returned the one he had given me at the restaurant. I had recognized the title when he first mentioned it. Another friend of mine had asked me to read the Afterword of this book several weeks before I even met Joe. I thought the coincidence of two of my best friends asking me to read the same book was interesting, so I got into it right away. Of course, I started with the Afterword. Remember, I always start a book at the ending! As I read those words I could feel the excitement rise within me. The man who wrote this book was talking about me! I know this sounds weird, but I recognized everything he was saying. I already "knew" what he had written and he explained things that I had wondered (about myself) for years and years. It was such a relief to read those words, to know that someone else had understood my feelings!

I called the first friend, and told him I had finally read the book he had recommended to me, and I told him how I came to read it. His comment to me was, "Recognize anything?" I could hear him smiling. He had known that I would really relate to the book and that its positive messages would be of help to me.

Shortly after Joe's visit to our house, things began to fall apart.

Twice in one week, in the month of March, 1992, I woke up beet red. My body was as red as a fire truck and I felt like I *was* on fire. Mentally, I felt wonderful, as though something great was about to happen. I was excited. But I was a little concerned about the redness, so I took my temperature to see if I had a fever. No fever, though. And, after a while, the redness began to subside. I was able watch it slowly leave my body, from head to toe, much like a thermometer goes down. "One more odd thing to note in my journal," I thought.

By the end of that week, James and I had noticed that the dog would no longer sleep in the bed with me. This was most unusual. I had been trying to get her out of our bed for years, and now I couldn't get her in! She would pace back and forth at the foot of our bed, whining and scratching. James would pick her up and put her in with me, but she would practically break her neck to get away. We were puzzled, to say the least. The topper to this came that weekend; James came to me and asked me to sit down. He said he had something important to tell me. We poured some coffee and sat down at the kitchen table. Then, James dropped a bomb on me. He said that he knew why the dog would no longer sleep with me and that seeing her act strange had made him remember. He told me that one night, earlier that week, he had been awakened by the violent movement of our waterbed. He said the waves were so huge that it nearly knocked him onto the floor and that he could see our dog flopping helplessly around the bed, moaning and whimpering. I was nowhere to be seen and he couldn't understand how I could have gotten out of the room so quickly if I had been the one to disturb the bed. He proceeded to roam around the house, searching for me. Before he left the room, he saw a tremendous bright, blue flash of light come through the bedroom door. He said that it had come from the back hallway, near the garage access door. Then, for reasons completely unknown to him, he decided to go back to bed. Sounds pretty crazy, doesn't it? It turned out that the night that he described was one of those nights during which I'd awoken all flushed with red and gripped with excitement. But it was what he told me next that really floored me.

James told me he believed that he had no business being in my life—no business being married to me. His exact words were that he "was a boat anchor around my neck." He told me that I didn't belong to him or anyone else and he was afraid he'd wake up one day to find me gone, forever. (I don't think he that meant I would leave him in the conventional way). My red flags went up right away. I really couldn't understand what he was saying. I asked him if he was trying to unload me with a bunch of UFO crap so that he could run off with some other woman and make me think it was somehow my fault. For some reason, I got the impression that he had been frightened by someone, or something. He was insistent that there was no other woman in the picture, and he insisted that he didn't want us to split. He was also adamant about how he felt, and he was certain he was right. I told him that if there was no other woman and if he really wanted to stay together then to just forget what he was worrying about—everything would be okay. He reluctantly agreed to drop the whole matter and we went on with the evening's business. Unfortunately, his feelings turned out to be quite prophetic.

Within a week of our conversation something else happened that seemed to confirm that a change was imminent. One morning I awoke covered with cut grass. James had mown the orchard the evening before. At first, I found myself cursing him, thinking that he had dragged grass through the house on his shoes. After I got out of the bed, though, I realized that there was no grass anywhere in the house—not even on his side of the bed. I looked into the bedroom mirror and was alarmed to find grass stuck to the back of my gown, on the back of my head and on my bare arms and legs! I couldn't figure out what had happened. I felt fine. Actually, I felt great, like those two days when I woke up red as a beetroot.

I got out the vacuum cleaner and, as I began to sweep the grass off the bed, I noticed that my fingers were starting to itch. I reached down to scratch them and realized that my wedding rings were gone! Where they had been, the skin had become red and had begun to peel. I became frantic that my rings were gone, and I tore the house apart looking for them. I even ripped open the sweeper bag, thinking that perhaps I'd sucked them up, accidentally. What in the hell was I going to tell James if he noticed they were gone? This was the *second* time rings James had given me wound up missing under mysterious circumstances! Was this a sign of some sort?

Three days later, while making our bed in the morning, I shook out the bedspread and accidently hit one of the stones on the window-ledge with a corner of the sheet, knocking it onto the bed. When I reached over to place the stone back on the ledge, there, in the exact spot the stone had been, were my wedding rings! The window-ledge had been the first place I'd looked when the rings first came up missing three days earlier. I thought perhaps I'd had taken off my rings in my sleep somehow and laid them on the ledge (the ledge was directly above the top of the bed). I had looked that ledge over very carefully at the time, and the rings were *definitely* not there. But now, there they were, in the most obvious place, a place I had already inspected three days before.

Our relationship deteriorated rapidly after this. I had become increasingly positive that something wonderful was about to happen and, despite the poor state of my personal life, I was in fairly good spirits. James was growing increasingly unnerved to the point where every little thing was eating away at him. He had always been rather moody, but he was getting worse by the day. On the one hand, I felt sorry for him; on the other hand, I couldn't let our relationship go on like this, for all of our sakes. I could never say that our unusual experiences destroyed our marriage—I suspect that it was doomed from the start—but surely they were a contributing factor.

On June 14, 1992, I left. The boys and I moved back to my parents' home—the house where it all started. Moving was such a pain in the rear end, but I felt such a sense of relief that I knew I had made the right decision.

Four days later, on June 18, 1992, my parents' home was hit by a tornado. Mother Nature has such a way with timing! We had just gotten unpacked, and the kids were in upheaval having just left their home, their friends, and their stepfather. Dad had just turned in his paperwork to officially retire after 35 years at the same job. His retirement was to go into effect in less than one week.

Thank God we all came through it safely. The house had minimal damage—a broken window, some shingles gone, some broken-up guttering, damaged evergreens, broken concrete sidewalk and steps, and a leaking roof. Our vehicles didn't fare so well. A sixty-five-foot beech tree that was twisted off at the trunk by the tornado, and flung through the air, had bored its way through my van and my mother's new car. They had just sent off the last payment two days earlier, and my van was free and clear, too.

Both vehicles were impaled and the tree landed within ten feet of where I was standing. I watched it come at me like a spinning spear. My life flashed before my eyes. I was in such a state of shock that I literally couldn't move. It happened so fast! Now, I know what an opossum feels like as he stares into oncoming headlights! All that saved my life that night were the two vehicles between me and the tree.

As the sun rose the next morning, we began to see just how lucky we had been. The whole front of the house was strewn with downed trees. Dad and I circled the property to inspect the damage. I just stood there, crying, feeling as if now I had lost everything I ever had, except my children and my family (the most important things). The van had been my final link to James. Finding it had been a dream come true and we had made a lot of plans for that van. But it had also become a reminder of how the marriage had failed, and it had been making me sad. The very afternoon of the storm, not long before it hit, I had been sitting on the front porch with my mom, looking at the van, feeling bad about the way things turned out with James and me. After it had been destroyed by the storm, mom remarked to me that at least it'd no longer be there to remind me. She also recognized that if those vehicles hadn't been where they were at that time, I wouldn't have been sitting there talking to her that day. Mom believed that nothing happens by chance—everything happens because it has to. Even if the reasons aren't immediately clear. I think she was right.

We didn't have electricity for several days after the tornado hit. Since we are on a well and septic system, we had no water or toilet, either. But we'd learned about this in the blizzard of '78, so we were prepared with a generator. Unfortunately, it had a tendency to run out of gas at the most inopportune times.

On the third night without power, I had a very unusual experience. When I had gone to bed, the generator was running to keep the refrigerator and freezer operational. Sometime during the night, it ran out of gas and we lost power. I heard Dad get up to refill the tank with fuel. As I lay there, in the dark, lonely and quiet, thinking about the last few days, I began to realize that I wasn't alone in the room. A soft glow appeared around the foot and sides of my bed, just barely bright enough for me to see. And then I noticed them, standing around my bed—the strangest crew of people I have ever seen. There were eight in all. Old, young, male, female people, all looking at me with varying degrees of concern and curiosity. Standing closest to me, at the head of the bed, was an old woman. She leaned into me and whispered in my ear, "Don't you remember us?" I lay there, as still as I could. Looking at her through the corner of my eye, I said to her, "No, I don't." Then she said, "Well, we don't actually look like this, but we know you've been through a lot recently. You've done very well through it all. We only chose to appear to you in this manner for your benefit. Look at me and you will remember." Then, she got *right* in my face, nose-to-nose. I didn't move, but I closed my eyes as tight as I could, and yelled out, loudly, "*No way* am I looking at you! Go away! I'm not in the mood for this right now! Buzz off!" She kept insisting that I look at her, but I kept on refusing. Finally, she said, "Very well. We know you are tired. We will leave you now, but we will be back. Be patient. Things will improve." Then, suddenly, I was alone. As fast as it all happened, they were gone. I felt incredibly strange. I was sure I had been awake through the whole thing. Suddenly, the generator kicked in and the lights came back on. I lay there for a few more minutes, trying to comprehend what had just happened. Finally, exhaustion got the best of me and I drifted off to sleep.

I awoke the next morning with the experience of the previous night still fresh in my mind. I told my family about it and then I called Budd Hopkins and Linda Moulton Howe. When I talked to Linda, I reminded her of the phone call I had made to her in January, when I had told her that this was the year my life would change and it would be wonderful.

I told her, "Well, I see the changes, now where's the 'wonderful' part?" I could hear her smile as she told me to be patient. It reminded me of what the old lady had said to me the night before. As it turned out, they were right.

On June 29, 1992, I had another "virtual reality" dream. This one was to give me great comfort. I was standing in front of a small pond. The water level was very low, but rising. I could see water pouring out of a large machine on the other side of the pond. The water began to ripple out in front of me and, before I knew what was going on, two men began to rise up out of the water about 20 feet in front of me. One of these men—tall, blonde, and well-built—*walked across the surface of the water*, right toward me. He told me they were returning water that they had taken to study and that I should come with him. I agreed, so he slipped a pair of tight-fitting rubber-like boots onto my feet and walked me across the surface of the pond, to the machine that was unloading the water. The other man followed behind, quietly.

Inside the machine, I was taken into a room with soft lighting. He sat me down and told me that I shared his heritage and that I should remember that he had always loved me, and always would. He also said that he had known my mother, and that she had been to this place, as well. When he finished talking to me, he took me back to where he had first seen me. Before he left, he told me that he would be back someday to check on me again, and to please not forget him this time. I woke up as soon as the dream was over. It left me feeling very warm, safe and at peace with the world.

The event of the night of June 30, 1983 awakened something in me that had lain dormant in the deep recesses of my mind. My spirit was somehow set free. From the latter part of 1983, well into 1987, I found I could do things of which I had never before been capable. Even more astounding was the drive with which I did them.

Previously, I was not inclined to be artistic or poetic. I believe that my newfound abilities came as a direct result of my experiences. The desire to share with others what I had created was like nothing I've ever experienced before or since. It felt as though I'd discovered these new abilities within to help others find it within themselves somehow.

Beginning in September of 1983, incredible images began appearing in my head, and I felt strongly compelled to put them down on paper for others to see. I began to make collages. I spent every penny I had on materials to make them, and, once I started working on one, I couldn't stop until it was finished. I knew when it was time to make a new design because I would feel very anxious and fidgety for a day or two before the actual work began. That was my cue to go to the dime store for construction paper and glue. Then, early in the morning—usually around 2 or 3am—I'd wake up, feeling shaky and sweaty, and I would know it was time to start.

It was during one such episode that I produced a couple of poems. In both cases, I was feeling very agitated and anxious a few days before they surfaced. I felt them inside me like steam in a whistle-kettle, gradually building. When I wrote them down, some of the pressure was released. I woke up out of a sound sleep to write them, and afterward I collapsed onto the bed and fell away, relieved, at last.

The following morning, I awoke to find all these chicken scratches on my note pad. I had to rearrange a few words and sentences for them to make any logical sense.

This is the first one I got. I call it,

Song for Per:

When I look into your eyes, I become you
I pass through to the inner core, which is the true self
Reaching in, I bathe in the warmth of your highest essence
I comfort and ease the coolness of your human emotions
I open your heart and your mind in the name of love
All memory we now and forever share
Fused by the power of our soul
We are all but one soul
Massive and eternal
One memory, one love
In the beginning, split with fear
We now struggle to learn, to return to the place
When we will come, once again
Together, forever

Debbie Jordan
1986

Here's the second one:

Prophet's Prayer

Why, oh why, must I be the one
To feel the light, yet share with none?
Understanding the human soul
Will, I fear, take its toll
Grant me strength to carry on
To be, again, with you, as one
Send to me what I've searched for so long
My fate fulfilled, my duty done
How long must I wait?
My patience wears thin
A lesson to learn before I begin?
You are my heart, my life you command
Yet all that must be, I cannot comprehend
The message is vague and yet just within reach
Am I not the pupil or is it I who must teach?

Debbie Jordan
1987

NINE

New Abilities

~

For many years now, I have exhibited abilities that have defied explanation. One winter night, when I was pregnant with my first child, my husband at the time, Chuck, had gone bowling with his father. They bowled every Wednesday on a league. I had gone to bed early. I wasn't feeling all that great—a normal side effect of my pregnancy.

Around midnight, I was awakened out of a sound sleep with a tremendous feeling of urgency. Something was wrong. I paced back and forth for at least ten minutes. It wasn't that I was worried about my husband returning late or anything like that—it was not unusual for him to arrive home until after 1:00am on bowling night. I felt strange. Different. I found myself drawn to the patio door, gazing out at seemingly nothing over the frozen lake.

Slowly, I began to realize that there was something wrong out there. So, I decided to go down to the lake and have a closer look. Here I was, generously pregnant, dressed only in my housecoat and slippers, tromping through the snow outside my apartment building, searching for the cause of my unease. Pretty crazy, right? What's new?

When I reached the edge of the lake, I could see nothing out of order. As I stood there, I was struck once again by a feeling of urgency and terror. I knew something was wrong—that someone was afraid—and I knew that I had to help them!

I still couldn't see a darn thing from where I was standing, so I decided to walk down the shore a little farther. As I passed by the next building, I could see that a truck had fallen into the lake. The front end was frozen in the ice and the bed was sticking up out of the slush. I could see footprints surrounding the vehicle, but they were so scrambled that I couldn't tell where they were headed.

It was then that my husband and his father arrived home and came walking around the building, looking for me. I pointed out the truck to them, excitedly, ignoring my husband's scolding for me being outside in the cold while pregnant. He said that whoever had wrecked the vehicle was probably out somewhere, trying to find a tow truck, and that I should quit worrying about it and come inside immediately. He should have known better than to boss-around a pregnant woman. I told him where to get off and that I would be in when I was ready. So, he and his dad reluctantly went back up to the apartment and left me there to continue my search.

I stood at the bank for several minutes, looking out over the frozen lake. I thought I heard someone call for help at point, but could see nothing. Then, I heard it again, and there was no mistaking it this time. I watched as a small, dark form surfaced out of the ice. That man must have mustered up every last ounce of his strength to drag himself out of the ice like that. I could barely hear his frozen voice crying out to me for help. I began screaming to him to hold on—that I'd find help as quick as I could. I yelled up to the building behind me for someone to call the rescue squad. A light went on in one of the apartments, and a head peeked out from behind the shade. But they offered no assistance. Instead they quickly shut off their light and closed their window! Damn, that made me mad!

I charged up the stairs to my apartment, grabbed the phone, and called 911. My husband had the stupidest look on his face. "I told you so!" I yelled, as I ran back outside. I had told the rescue squad to meet me on the other side of the lake, as the man appeared to be closer to that bank than to mine. By the time I got over there, they already had him halfway out. The rescue worker asked me if I had been the one who called. I told him yes, and I asked him if the guy would be all right. He assured me that he would be okay once they got him warmed up a little, but that if I hadn't found him when I did, it would have been a different story. I thought, "I've got news for you, Buddy—*he* found *me*!" The "ice man" looked up at me from the arms of his rescuer and whispered a barely audible "thank you." I was just grateful that he was still alive and that I had found the source of my unease that night. I walked off into the darkness, around the lake, and back to my warm apartment. I never even told the rescuer my name. My job was done. I needed sleep!

A great many changes occurred for me during the early-1990s, and I began to spend more time with my friends. Thank God for them. They helped me get through the roughest parts of my personal life.

My friend Joe and I decided to make a run down to St. Louis to see Forest. Joe and Forest had never met, and I wanted to introduce them. We had made plans to hang out around the campfire, and to enjoy other's company out in nature. While we were at Forest's house, he had a visitor. A friend of his stopped in—a physicist named Dave. He brought with him some experiments that Forest wanted to conduct on me and a couple of other women in the St. Louis area who also had experiences with UFOs. I liked Dave. He didn't just accept things at face value. He checked things out very thoroughly, like a true scientist.

Joe and I had been out in Forest's back yard, having a smoke and admiring the wooded lot behind his house. When I went back in, I noticed that Dave had arrived. He, Forest, and the two women were seated around the dining room table. I also noticed that the two women were passing a small paper bag back and forth between themselves. I surmised that they were trying to figure out what was in the bag. This was one of Dave's experiments, and he was observing closely as the girls worked.

The moment I walked into the house, I felt very heavy. As I sat at the table, watching, I began to feel the familiar burn and tingle of my physical response to magnets. A year or so earlier I had participated in an experiment with a researcher from my neighboring state of Ohio, and I had realized that I had the ability to *physically feel* the nearby presence of strong magnets.

During the Ohio experiment, I was blindfolded. Another person would then move a super-magnet around my head and body without actually touching me, taking note of physical and psychological reactions. I was also hooked up to a bio-feedback monitor that would record any miniscule changes in skin temperature, skin moisture, or involuntary muscle movements. The sensations I felt during that test completely blew my mind. I was extremely surprised that I had felt anything! I didn't expect any reaction at all. So, when I first began to feel the heat and the tingling, I ignored it. As the test progressed, I could feel the sensations increase to the point that I could barely tolerate it. I also began to feel a heightened sense of anxiety well up inside of me, for no apparent reason. As the physical feelings increased, so did the anxiety. Just as the feelings were about to peak, I suddenly felt as though I were being pulled out of my body, through the top of my head. At that point, I stopped the test. I just couldn't take any more. I realized I had felt those feelings before, several times. I had those feelings right before paranormal and UFO experiences. I had also felt the same sensations during an MRI test that was conducted a few years earlier. The technician performing the test had attributed the feelings to claustrophobia. I assured her I didn't have that problem and that I had felt funny as soon as I walked into the building. She must have thought I was nuts. I didn't realize that the magnet was affecting me, and I'm sure she didn't realize it, either.

Now, here I was, sitting in my friend's dining room, feeling those same sensations once again. I knew that there was only one thing that would cause this—and so I knew what was in the bag. I leaned over the table, got Forest's attention, and mouthed the words, "I know what's in the bag." He whispered back to me, "what?" You should have seen his face when I told him it was a magnet. Priceless! He grabbed Dave's arm and told him to listen to me. When I told Dave that there was a magnet in his little bag and how I knew it, he, too, was blown away. That was the first time I had any real witnesses to my suspected new abilities.

I had been feeling "different," for lack of a better way to describe it. I had, in the past, exhibited some unusual abilities, such as bending metal objects with a light touch, ending people's sentences for them, and being able to *feel* certain sounds. But this was different. I noticed that recently I had begun to dream in color, and in 3D. These vivid, virtual reality dreams were incredible experiences. They always seemed to happen just when I was about to fall asleep yet was still aware of my surroundings. The major difference between those and my regular dreams is that I was no longer merely watching them unfold. I was actually *in* the dream. I had full use of all my senses, and my abilities were limitless. I now understand what people mean when they talk of out-of-body experiences, and I wonder if what they are really experiencing is simply this heightened state of dream reality. I use the term "reality" because it seems to me that this state in which I sometimes find myself *is* another reality—an altered reality.

Here's an example of one of my particularly vivid "V.R." dreams. I had just lain down on the couch to watch some old television series on "Nick at Nite." I think it was an old *Dick Van Dyke Show* rerun (I love those old sitcoms!). I could still hear the T.V. when, all of a sudden, I felt myself start to slip away. With a rather loud "swoosh" sound in my head, I found myself floating in space. Just me and my Dr. Denton's. I was startled at first, but quickly began to enjoy myself. I decided to turn back and look at the Earth passing behind me. As I turned my head to look over my right shoulder, I could see this huge cylindrical object headed toward me in a flat spin. It had what appeared to be gold appendages of some kind, one on each side, which I compared to those fancy, new-fangled windshield wiper blades. As it got closer to me, I could see that it was at least as big as a motor home or school bus. As it passed by me, its end spun around towards me and I could see that the end of it looked as if it had been blown out. Actually, it looked like it had just been opened with an old-fashioned can opener. There was a little bit of what looked like vapor spurting out of the darkened, open end of this thing. This image really gave me the creeps and I woke up instantly. The first, most insistent thing in my mind was that I had to call someone. Anyone would do, just so long as I used the telephone. I called K.O. Bless his heart, it must have been 2:00am and I'm sure I woke him up. I felt like an idiot, but he seemed to understand. I was really wound up after this and it took several hours for me to finally get some sleep.

The next morning, I called Linda Moulton Howe and told her all about it. When I told my friend Liz, in Pennsylvania, about my dream, she nearly came through the phone at me! It turned out she'd had *the very same dream* on the *very same night*! She had written hers down and had called John Carpenter and told him about it before we even talked. Anyway, it felt like my mind was somehow expanding, and it even seemed to be having an effect on my I.Q.

I had to obtain a copy of my high school transcripts when I enrolled in Cosmetology school. As I was cleaning out my cedar chest one afternoon, I ran across my records and had a look. I was surprised to see that my I.Q. had scored at 111. Not too shabby, but I was certainly no rocket scientist, and I could live with that. Later, my boyfriend talked me into taking a test for a group called Mensa—the international organization for people who score in the upper two percent of the country on their I.Q tests. I had goofed around with some of their practice tests in the *OMNI Magazine* and had no problem with any of them. Because I already had the scores from my transcripts, I was reluctant to try. Obviously 111 isn't in the top two percent. K.O. reasoned to me that this would be the perfect opportunity to see if anything had indeed changed, since I was feeling so different these days.

I agreed to the test and was shocked by the results, which placed me in the top *one* percent on the California Standard Mental Maturity Test, while the Cattell B Intelligence Test scored my I.Q. at 141. Additionally,

I scored in the top one-half percentile in spatial relations. Naturally, my first question was, "How could someone's I.Q. jump 30 points since the age of 15?" All I have been able to come up with is that either I.Q tests are worthless and we should stop using them to label people, or I was in a really poor state of mind when I took the first tests in junior high school. It seemed that my experiences were expanding not only my consciousness but also my intellect.

~

Since I was now living with my parents again, I decided to take on a few more speaking engagements. Mom would take care of my children and I wouldn't have to answer to a spouse anymore. Besides, I needed to get away from everything for a while. I had accepted a request to talk to the Gulf Breeze Research Team in Pensacola, Florida. The sun and beautiful white sand beaches sounded pretty good! I knew one of the members of the group very well and was looking forward to seeing her again. As a matter of fact, I would be staying with her at her home. I thought it would be fun, sort of like a grown-up girls' slumber party. Some uninvited guests crashed our party, though.

When I arrived in Pensacola that Friday, I was pooped! I really hate to fly. There just has to be a better way to travel. My ears and sinuses weren't meant to fly and I have my suspicions about the science of aerodynamics. I really do know better than to trust my life to the precarious balance between lift and drag! I find it hard to believe there's nothing between me, in this heavy piece of metal, and the ground, except for a few clouds and about 30,000ft of air!

My first night in Vicki's house was wonderful. The bed was comfy, and I was ready for it. Saturday was a hectic day, sight-seeing and, as my father so quaintly used to call it, shoplifting (of course, I mean shopping for souvenirs. The prices I paid made me feel like I was the one being robbed!).

Saturday night was spent on my very first sky-watch. What a neat experience it was. Except for the mosquitoes, the company was excellent and I made a lot of good friends that night. I ran into a few old friends, too. Dr. Bruce Macabee was there on the beach with a couple of fellow scientists and a whole bunch of sophisticated recording instruments. I couldn't begin to tell you all that he had there that night. I'm no scientist, and I had no idea what most of that stuff did. I did recognize the camcorders, the telescopes and the 3D camera equipment. And I saw a van filled to the brim with recording devices. There were a few antennas on the roof of the van and I noticed a dish of some kind, also. I do know that one of their instruments could pick up and record each sweep of the radar that passed over us from one of the local air bases.

A few of us (the ones who couldn't take the 'skeeters anymore) ventured down to the beach, right next to the water. We set our lawn chairs in a small circle and all began to focus our minds on a similar idea, calling 'Bubba' in. (Bubba was their pet name for the red lights and other objects they see in the sky down there often). It was peaceful and cool, and the mosquitoes couldn't handle the wind coming in off the waves.

After a short while, I began to feel the familiar burn and tingle of my response to strong magnets. Immediately, I turned to my friend Vicki and said, "Somebody's here, checking us out... closer than you think, too." Within one minute, a gal named Pat came running down the sand dune from the parking lot where everyone else was watching, to tell us that several of the people on the lot, including Dr. Macabee, had seen a small, white ball of light whizz overhead. They said the light seemed to be moving in a sort of "dash-dash, stop and go" way, and that it had come across above our heads as we sat on the beach, moving from left to right above us in the parking lot. It appeared to be about twenty-feet off the ground. At the very moment they spotted the light, and I had felt the magnet response, one of the scientists with Dr. Macabee reported that he had picked up an unusual square-shaped wave on one of his instruments.

Everyone thought it interesting that not only did they see this thing with their own eyes, but also that I felt it, and their instruments had detected an anomalous reading at the same time. Even if there was a rational explanation for what the instrument picked up, I still think it noteworthy that I could *feel* it right before they saw it (I did not see the light).

We finally got back to Vicki's very early on Sunday morning. I was dead tired and eaten up with bug bites. To help stop the itching and to wash off the bug spray, I took a quick shower before crashing. Once I lay down, I couldn't go to sleep. I don't know if I was overly tired or overly excited about the events earlier that day on the beach. I picked up a magazine and began to flip through it. Nothing puts me to sleep faster than reading. I have wimpy eyes.

While I was reading, something caught my eye. I looked up and saw a small, white ball of light up in the corner of the room, to my right.

At first, I thought it might be a reflection of my reading light on the oscillating fan in the room. I watched the fan and the light and realized there was no connection. As I looked directly at the light, it shot across the room, stopped, momentarily, over Vicki's desk, and then shot right over my head, and to my left. Then, it was gone. I didn't feel frightened by this little incident, and soon I was fast asleep. The last thing I remembered was hearing several conversations going on in my room.

The next morning, I told Vicki about what I had seen in the room a few hours earlier. She was quite excited about it and she made me promise that, if I ever saw anything like that again in her house, I would come and tell her, right away. She wanted to see it, too. She said that she had heard several strange noises in the house at around the same time that I saw this light, and we wondered if there was a connection.

Monday was another hectic day of sightseeing and frolicking on the beach. That evening, we had another sky-watch. As before, we were up very late, and when I returned to Vicki's I had to take another shower to combat the itchy mosquito bites and wash away the bug spray. As I climbed into bed, I turned on the reading light and began to browse the magazine I'd started the previous night. After a couple of minutes, I began to notice a soft, bluish-white glow coming from behind my left shoulder. There was a window directly behind the head of my bed; I assumed it was just a car light of some kind—headlights, or something. When I began to feel that familiar burning, tingling magnetic response again, I realized something was wrong with my headlight theory. I wondered whether the reading light was reflecting off of the oscillating fan, throwing it back onto the shiny paper of the magazine, and then over my shoulder. I tried several experiments with holding the paper different ways, but to no avail. I tried to rationalize the situation, but nothing was working. The glow began to pulsate and grow larger with each throb. I thought, "I should get Vicki. She wants to see this." With that thought, the glow stopped. I sat there for a moment, waiting for what might come next. I wasn't about to look over my shoulder. I had the distinct impression that, if I did, I might see something I really didn't want to see—closer to me than I really wanted it to be.

After a minute or two, I decided that there was no point in waking Vicki. Whatever it was had probably split. Precisely after I thought this, something whipped around my left shoulder. It appeared to be many small beams of blue and white light—blue at the core and white around the edges, in alternating fashion. "Fingers" of light, is how I described it. It literally slapped me across the left side of my face and neck. The force was so strong that I felt stunned. I also felt a small electrical shock, and I could feel a burning, numb sensation on the whole left side of my face. It felt as if the thing were going to wrap itself around my whole head and not let go! (There were red marks on my neck and jaw the next morning). Immediately, I said, out loud, "Okay! I'll get Vicki, for Christ's sake!" With that, it let go of me and was gone.

I jumped off the bed and made my way through the dark house to Vicki's room. I didn't know where the light switch was in the kitchen, so I stood there for a moment. Then, I said softly, "Vicki?" As soon as the words left my mouth, there came Vicki, dashing out of her room, yelling, "Don't tell me, girl, I saw it, too! Blue and white lights came up from under my bedroom door, they looked like rays, and then I could see it move down the hall toward your room!" I just stood there, my mouth agape, not knowing whether to breathe that next breath or drop over like a fly. I felt as if I were in a daze, half there, half somewhere else.

Vicki's husband, Danny, came out of the room right after her. Both of them, their eyes as big as saucers, listened as I told them what had happened in my room. Interestingly, Vicki and I both had heard a strange rattling noise in the utility room, near the dog pen, and movement throughout the house, as if someone was bumping up against furniture as they passed through. I thought it was Vicki or Danny, and they thought it was me. It was none of us. (The following day, one of Vicki's dogs became very ill, which was of serious concern to Vicki).

We made our way back to my room. I showed them where all this had happened and, as I retold the event, we all got more and more creeped out. Eventually, we all wound up sitting on my bed, covers half pulled up around our necks, looking for the boogieman out of the corner of our eyes. I must admit, I was the biggest weenie of all. There I was, in Florida, to talk to a large group of people about how I had finally overcome my fears, wanting to show them how they could do the same, and I was the most freaked out of all. I felt like a true jerk! I was never so embarrassed in my whole life! I was taken so off guard by this whole thing that I think I was more in shock than anything else. I also think that there may have been more to this whole thing than I remember because, the next morning, I made a strange discovery. My trusty Timex wind-up watch was running thirty minutes slow. It had kept good time for ten years, but somehow, that night, it lost half an hour. I felt a strange connection to Florida after that, and I still can't shake it. I miss it very much.

After agonizing over how I would ever get any sleep that night, I decided to have Vicki drive me over to K.O.'s hotel room. I knew it was very late, but I had woken him before, and somehow, I knew he would understand. He did.

K.O. was quite alarmed to see us knocking at his door so early in the morning, but he graciously let us in. We told him what had happened and, right away, he began recording the whole thing for future reference. So efficient. I remembered looking in his mirror and telling him that I didn't look like me anymore. I could see something different looking back at me in my reflection. Boy, was I a wreck! He could see that I was in shock and he noticed that my eyes looked unusually bright. "Glowing," was the word he used. He thought it was so unusual that he broke out his camcorder and videotaped me. Then, he fixed up the extra bed for me. I fell onto it, rolled myself up in a tight ball, reminded myself that he was there, that he would keep me safe, and then I really crashed hard. I was fried!

On Monday night, without telling anyone, K.O. decided that he would spend the night outside Vicki's house. He was very protective of me, even then. He felt that he might see something, and I guess he did. He parked his car on a side street so that he could have a good view of my room and of her utility room. He got very sleepy, despite tons of coffee, and found himself nodding off a lot. At one point, however, he remembered seeing two small lights appear along the side of her house, just below the utility room windows. They both winked out before he could get his camcorder up to catch them on film. He said they weren't much bigger than white Christmas tree lights. Inside the house, it was pretty quiet.

I gave my talk on Tuesday. It went really well and when I told them about what had just happened the night before, everyone wanted me to spend the night with them! Now, wouldn't you have expected the exact opposite? What a group!

The entire Gulf Breeze Research Team decided to camp out around Vicki's house that night. Each one had their post, and I think they had the whole house surrounded. I felt kind of bad that they were going to miss a whole night's sleep because of me, but they wouldn't take no for an answer. I sure felt safe that night! But, perhaps, I shouldn't have.

I went to bed at 1:20am. The window was open, the lights and the TV were off. At 1:30am. I was abruptly jolted out of a deep sleep by a very strong magnetic response. I lay there, stunned. Shortly, I began to drift back to sleep. Again, at exactly 1:40am, it happened again. This time I got out of bed, lit a cigarette, and turned on the T.V. I knew the light from the T.V. would impair the observers outside, but I did it anyway. After I had finished my smoke, I went back to bed and fell asleep rather easily. At 4:00am, I woke up, abruptly, sitting straight up in the bed. As I looked around the room, trying to regain my composure, I slid myself down into the bed slowly, thinking to myself, "Wow, What a trip."

The next morning, Vicki told me that at 3:55am, one of the watchers, Dave, had discovered that his car battery had gone dead. At that time, the whole G.B.R.T. was hovering around Dave's car, trying to get it started—at nearly exactly the same time I woke up sitting straight up in bed, bewildered and confused. Dave's battery would never hold a charge after that. It was destroyed, and he had to replace it.

~

In March of 1993, I was invited to participate in the making of a pilot for a possible new television series on the UFO subject. The filming was in Daytona Beach, Florida. While I was there, something interesting happened.

Budd Hopkins had also been invited to appear on the show. Over the telephone, I had told Budd about a then-recent experience of mine in which I had been freezing cold and unable to get warm. I finally had to abandon my basement bedroom for the couch upstairs, where it was warmer. Sometime early in the morning, I had been awakened by a blonde man who asked me if I was still cold. I told him, "No, in fact, I'm burning up."

He said, "Here, let me help you." With that, he proceeded to pull off my sweatpants and socks, fold them up neatly and put them on the coffee table next to the couch. Then he began to talk to me. I cannot remember what he said exactly, but I remember at one point saying to him, "Hey, one of your eyes is weird! The pupil is diamond-shaped, and it moves when you talk to me. Are you talking to me with your eye?" (What a dumb question!). He looked at me like I was stupid and said, "Well, of course I am! Don't you remember you can do this, too?"

I said, in return, "Oh, yeah, right. Whatever." Then he talked to me for a little while longer. I just remembered saying, "Yeah, uh huh, okay, yeah." I can't remember what he said to me. The next thing I know, it's morning and there are my sweatpants and socks, neatly folded, lying on the coffee table.

I drew a picture of the man that night in my hotel room in Daytona, where I was staying for the TV show, and I was going to give it to Budd the next day. After I had finished the picture, I set it up against the toaster to get a head-on view of it, to see how it looked. The T.V. caught my eye. There was a comedienne onscreen that looked just like Judy Garland. I loved Judy Garland. I was fascinated by her, and woke up K.O. to see her. He had been lying across the bed, in his street clothes, and had dozed off.

As K.O. and I watched the T.V., I standing next to the bed, he lying across it with his chin on his fists, I saw a small, white light appear between us and the T.V. I couldn't believe my eyes! I watched it move slowly across the screen, past the kitchen chair and over to my drawing. It had some kind of tail trailing behind it. Like a jet contrail. This thing moved like a swimming tadpole! I had never seen anything like this in my whole life! When it reached my drawing, it stopped, hesitated a moment and then just disappeared. K.O. had seen me tracking something and asked me what I was seeing. I kept rubbing my eyes, thinking that would make it go away. I jumped and yelled, "Whoa! Did you see that?" I thought K.O. was going to fall off the bed! He yelled, "What? I didn't see it! What was it?" I couldn't believe he didn't see it. It passed right in front of his face. He had let his eyes droop shut for just a minute and had missed the whole thing! Dammit to hell!

On the flight home, as we sat and ate our peanuts, the whole back-end of the plane filled suddenly with a bright, flash of white light. I was next to the window. It was dark and I was getting sleepy. I turned my head to look out of the blackened window, closed my eyes for just a second, and then it happened. The flash was so bright that it came through my closed eyes, bright enough to startle me. At first, I thought it was lightning. I could see that the man in the seat in front of us had apparently seen it, too. He was looking around with this puzzled expression on his face. K.O. had also seen it, and at first thought it was a reflection from the peanut wrapper of the man next to us. Quickly, he realized that it was much too bright to have been merely a reflection. We waited for more flashes, thinking it might be lightning, but none ever came. That was the only one.

I looked over at K.O. and said, "Whoa man, what if we land at Indianapolis International and find out the name's been changed to Weircook?" (That was supposed to be a joke. Weircook was the name of Indianapolis International Airport, long ago). Given what I already know about my crazy life, *nothing* would surprise me!

~

I have long been prone to having "premonitions," especially since the incident of June 30, 1983. As I got older and more experienced, I began to pay more attention to them, and to recognize the difference between what were just my own random thoughts and these "lessons" or, in some cases, "warnings."

Right before we moved from our old farmhouse into the house of our current residence, I had a strange premonition that saved the lives of my beloved pet birds. It was 2012; we had just sold a 3500 square foot, three-story farmhouse with two acres of land, and we were downsizing. It was a daunting task, considering we had nearly thirty-years' worth of possessions that belonging to three adults. It eventually required two full-sized dumpsters, several trips to the Goodwill, and two garage sales. What a pain in the ass *that* was! This was the beginning of the process of breaking me of my desire for material belongings. We were moving into a 1740-square-foot ranch-style home. A good home to retire in. Everything was on one floor; there were no stairs to have to negotiate and the yard was so small it could easily be tended to with a push-mower. Condensing our possessions was difficult.

At that time, we also had four birds in our care. I had an Umbrella Cockatoo named Casper, a Blue Front Amazon named Ozzie, and two Cockatiels, named Elvis and Buddy. The "aviary" was a mostly unused dining room that was perfect for them. It contained their mess and allowed them freedom to explore the house. I had raised Casper from a chick, hand feeding her and teaching her how to play with her toys and talk. She was funny, loving, smart and *loud*! Ozzie was Daddy's bird. He got Ozzie after Mom passed away, for the company, and, when Daddy passed, I inherited him. He never really got over Dad, and I have a scar on my upper lip to prove how much he didn't like me. Buddy and Elvis had come to us many years prior from another bird-loving friend whose birds had babies. In the town where I lived, I was known as the "bird lady."

I had fully intended to take all the birds with us for the move—all the way up until about two-weeks prior to closing on the new place. I had intended to use one of the extra bedrooms as the bird room. I had plans of turning it into a nifty aviary, and eventually we were going to build a sort of "Florida Room," with lots of windows, and a door that could close when Casper got loud. One day, while cleaning the cages, I suddenly heard a voice sounding out, loudly. It said, "They *cannot* move to the new house." I stopped and turned to see who said it, but I was alone.

As I continued to clean that day, I continued to hear that same voice, saying the same thing: "The birds *cannot* live in the new house."

How could I possibly move into my new home without my beloved birds? They were my children, since my kids had grown up and moved out, especially Casper. She used to wrap her huge wings around my shoulders and lick me on the neck to show me she loved me. She cooed and clucked at me like I was her mommy, because I *was*. But I could not ignore that voice. It was relentless. I finally told my husband that the birds could not come to live with us in the new house and that I was going to have to find them new homes before we moved. He looked at me like I was crazy. He loved them too, but he knew I was attached to them even more so them him. "Good luck with that," he said. "Good luck trying to find homes for them in two weeks."

Miracle of all miracles, I *did*! I had been telling everyone I knew that I had to find homes for my birds before we moved. I couldn't explain why, but I was hoping that, if I threw it out there, the universe would help me. Strangely enough, the lady who I was buying the house from, of all people, had a brother who lived in Florida, and he had a male Cockatoo that was his *life*, and it just so happened that he was looking for a mate for his bird. Arrangements were made and he drove all the way up here to take Casper back to Florida. He showed me pictures of the house and of the area where Casper would be homed; it was like a bird paradise. I felt comforted that she was going to have a good life and that she'd be loved by him as I had loved her. My stepson, who also lived in Florida, agreed to take Ozzie. He had bonded with him when he was up visiting. So, his half-brother picked up Ozzie, cage and all, and drove him to the Sunshine State. My stepson and Ozzie are besties now; they go everywhere together. Occasionally, I get pictures and videos of the two of them and it does my heart good.

I had placed an ad on Craigslist for a caretaker for the Cockatiels. The first person to respond was the mother of twin teenage girls who lived in a city south of us by about forty miles. After vetting the family, Elvis and Buddy went to live with the teenage sisters. The girls were aspiring veterinarians and wanted to have an experience caring for birds, with the help of their mother, of course. They sent me pictures of the girls and the birds and they all seemed to be happy and healthy. So, when we moved into the new house in August of 2013, we came *sans* birds.

In November 2013, just three months later, the house was completely destroyed by an F3 tornado. The mystery voice was correct: the birds could *not* live in that house. They *would all* have been killed. The moral of this story: *Pay attention!*

TEN

Changes

~

I wish you could have known me when I was younger. You would never have recognized me today. I had been plagued by depression and anxiety for as long as I can remember. When I was sixteen, my parents took me to see a psychiatrist. I had around five visits with him during the course of eighteen months. He wasn't much help. Most of what I remember from those visits are conversations about the effectiveness of the nerve pills he had prescribed to me, and creepy questions he would ask, like if anybody had touched me in a sexual way since our last consultation.

My self-image was low; I had an overwhelming inferiority complex. I had struggled with obesity since I was young and that certainly didn't make my life any easier. Sadly, it was food that became my "drug" of choice as a way of coping with my anxiety, but of course it only made things even harder.

At various stages throughout my life, the problems I was wrestling with manifested in the form of physical symptoms. Colitis, irritable bowel syndrome, obesity, nail biting, hyperventilation, gastroenteritis, reflux esophagitis, palpitations; the list goes on. All of this complicated my life even more. The doctors who saw me growing up must have thought me one pitiful little girl. Many of them probably wondered if I had been the victim of some kind of abuse while I was growing up. I guess, in a way, I was.

I look back on these last few years and I feel that I'm not the same person, that it was a different life entirely. "Who was that frightened, backward soul?"

I can't say that my experiences with these alien beings have caused the positive changes in my life (I use the word "alien" in the broadest sense—I don't know *what* they are or *where* they come from). Perhaps some of the changes in me were inadvertent side effects of the telepathic communication. Perhaps experiencing these traumatic events forced me into rising above it all, to change and to grow. Perhaps these qualities were already bred into me and that was why "they" were attracted to my people in the first place. I really don't have an answer for this. Budd always stressed to me, "Don't give 'them' the credit for what *you* did for yourself." It took a while for me to grasp what he was saying. But I do now. At the end of the day, all I can really do is live with it and make it work for me as best I can. I do know that I wouldn't change one thing about what I have been through, except maybe having them wait until I was older before they began. If I had been given the option of choosing whether or not to have these experiences, and if I knew then what I know now, I would have chosen to have them with the stipulation that I could fully remember them—understand their purpose and have at least some say as to what would be done to me. A couple of nice clear Kodak moments and a few scraps of anomalous metal for analysis would have been nice, too. I don't think I would have been able to reach my current level of consciousness without them—the experiences, that is. But perhaps my not knowing—not remembering—was all part of the plan, part of the program. Perhaps if I had remembered everything from the start, the results would have been different.

A very close friend of mine, who is also a UFO researcher, once asked me how I could not be angry and bitter toward whatever it is that's been messing with me and my family. He felt that they had used me like a lab animal against my will and that they didn't seem to care about the effects it would have on me, psychologically and physically. I asked him how he could be so sure that's how it really was—that I really was used and then dumped, with no regard for my personal health and wellbeing. Maybe we don't understand their ways, their version of concern or compassion. I was *there* and I wasn't even sure. I politely accused him of being slightly closed-minded.

Doctors vaccinate children for protection against all manner of horrible diseases. The shot hurts and the child cries. The older, wiser adult knows it was for the child's own good, and yet has no way of making the child understand this. He hopes that, as the child grows older, he will understand and know that the doctor meant no harm; that he was acting only in the child's best interests. How was my well meaning friend so sure that what was done to me wasn't for my own good, or the good of my species? I could have chosen to look at the whole situation from his point of view. I could have allowed myself to feel violated and used, angry and bitter, but what good would that do anyone, especially me? I believe that if we allow ourselves to stew in our own negative emotions, we will create negative reactions to that response. Just as our bodies respond to positive reactions by feeling energetic and strong, I believe we can make ourselves feel weak and tired, lowering our immunity to disease and attracting more negativity. We lose control of ourselves, our health, our state of mind and our lives. Did I really want to live my whole life feeling bad over something I may have misunderstood? Was it really worth making myself sick over? Or, should I try to look for an alternative response? One that might benefit me and could possibly help others to feel better, too.

Did I want to choose the constructive path, or the destructive path? Being a fairly intelligent, reasonable person, I choose to feel that the aliens' treatment has been beneficial to me. I don't allow my feelings to eat me alive. After all, as I've said before, I can't always choose the situations I find myself in, but I can choose how I respond to them. In this sense, I will always be in control of my life. I have begun to look at the human mind as a computer. And I am the programmer. I can program my mind to take me anywhere I want to be in life, so I can be anything I want to be, for me. When I came to this realization, the experiences began to change. They moved from the physical (the scars, the mark in the yard, the physical exams, etc.) to the psychological, the spiritual. It took a long time for me to shift to this new mode of thinking. I was never really as bitter as one might expect I would be, but I was terribly frightened. With my new-found sense of self-control, I have discovered new strength and an easing of the fear. It's amazing how much more clearly you can think when you're not as afraid of what you must think about. I realize how strong the human mind can be—so much so that I have learned never to trust in my memories of the experiences 100 percent. I realize that the mind can do many things in order to protect itself. I can be highly skeptical of my own memories, but I have learned to trust in me. I have faith in myself and my instincts, and, of course, in God. The more I trust in these, the stronger I get. When realizing your own encounters, keep in mind, all is not as it appears to be. Also, remember this: most people I've met who worry about whether they have gone crazy usually have not. The ones who think that *they* are "normal" and *everyone else* is crazy that are the ones who I watch out for!

It helps to keep notes on everything strange that happens. It also helps to remember that every bump and bruise, every weird little thing you notice, does not necessarily mean that "they" have been messing with you again. It's important to keep your perspective in all this. You can't imagine how much clearer things can become once they are written down. Re-reading your journal is like watching a movie three or four times. Each time you watch it, you pick up something new that you missed the time before; at least, I do. I will suddenly remember something new about the experience, something new about me. Sometimes, a more prosaic explanation will make itself clear to you after the initial shock has passed and you calm down a little. Keeping journals can actually help to explain a strange experience after a little time has passed.

~

On more than one occasion, I have experienced what I call "abductee burnout." It happens because you can only talk and think about this stuff so much. Pretty soon, you'll feel like your head will burst if you say or hear the words "abductee," "alien," or "terrified" even one more time. It can be extremely stressful to relive the feelings of fear and helplessness, even the physical pain of the experiences and the feelings of embarrassment at the ridicule that people like myself so often endure. Whenever I experienced these burnouts, I would withdraw. I would just back off it all for a while. I would refuse to talk about it, or read about it, and, if I saw something on TV about it, I would turn it off. Eventually, something would pull me back into it all again, but the reprieves were nice while they lasted.

Most people don't seem to realize that we didn't ask for this to happen to us. We're just trying to understand it, to understand "Why us?" Sometimes I would get angry and find myself yelling out into the dark night sky, "Why don't you just leave me alone? I don't want this life; I don't want this change. Please, I just want to be like normal people!" I didn't want the changes at first. Even though the changes were for the better, they were uncomfortable because they were new to me. Sometimes, even good changes are scary if they are unfamiliar. The best medicine is to talk about it. There are people who will listen without ridicule or judgment. Just being able to talk about it releases a lot of pressure. I believe that once you have found the inner strength to reach out to someone else and talk about something that bothers you, then half the battle has been won.

I can't give you any advice about how to stop the experiences. I don't know how to do that, and I no longer feel that I need to know. But this much I do know: I have learned to cope with my experiences—to integrate them into my life and to find some inner peace. I can also tell you about how it feels to be under hypnosis, for those of you who are considering it as a tool for exploring your own experiences. At first, I was scared to be hypnotized. Between what I had seen on television and what my sister had gone through when she tried it for weight loss, I wanted no part of it.

Hypnosis was nothing like I had imagined. Have you ever been on the verge of sleep when the phone rings? You jump up to answer it and it takes a minute for you to realize who you are talking to and where you are. That's the super-relaxed state in which I found myself while under hypnosis. For the first couple of sessions I found it hard to relax, but it wasn't too long before I started to feel more comfortable. When I realized that I was in control, I found I could let go a little more. Heck, the first time I ever had hypnosis, I didn't even know I was under until I woke up to find that almost two hours had passed. It seemed like fifteen minutes! If your therapist died during a session, the worst thing that would happen would be that you'd fall asleep and wake up a few hours later feeling refreshed and good... until you found out your therapist had croaked! If you decide to undergo hypnotherapy, please try to find an experienced and knowledgeable hypnotherapist, and be sure that you really want to do it. I come from the old school of thought: "If it ain't broke, don't fix it." If you are not having problems sleeping, health problems, or other problems that are seriously affecting your life, think hard before you decide to possibly open a can of worms. Even though I have yet to fully recall of the events of the night of June 30, 1983, I will not be seeking any further hypnosis for it. I figure that, when I am ready to remember it, it will come back to me in full.

I've been very fortunate in that I have always had the support of my family and friends. I realize that, for many people like me, there is no support. It must be even harder for those people. That's one of the reasons I wanted to write this book—perhaps the most important reason. I want to pass along to you some of what I have been blessed with. I feel that part of what I am here to do is to help people—to teach people how to cope with their own "impossible" experiences. It has only just begun. We have a come a long way, but we have a long way to go. I want you to realize that if *I* can come through this intact, stronger than ever, then so can you. What I have to say has nothing to do with

New Age philosophies or religious beliefs. It's just an alternative way of thinking. I have no interest in starting a cult, in or cultivating a following of any kind. That's the last thing I want. I just want people to know they are not alone in their experiences of extraordinary contact. You are acknowledged. You are heard. You are understood.

My feelings on just about everything—from life itself to death—have changed since our family was investigated and our experiences have become public. Through all the questions I have been asked, all the interviews with neighbors, family and friends, all the medical testing, psychological testing, voice stress testing, employer interviews, and everything else I have agreed to in the name of research, I have changed. I have learned, and I have grown.

~

I had a near-death experience (NDE) when I gave birth to my first son. Somehow, I feel it was connected to my other unusual experiences. It was not a conventional NDE; by which I mean that there was no white light at the end of a tunnel for me. Nor were there angels. No Devil, no God. (Nor were there aliens, surprisingly!)

I had to give birth to my son through emergency C-section after my kidneys failed as a result of a disease called eclampsia. I was semi-comatose by the time I was put under for the delivery. Suddenly, I could hear my doctor yelling at me to fight. His voice, and those of the other fifteen people in the delivery room, began to fade, then get louder, then fade again. With a loud swooshing sound, I found myself trapped in what appeared to be a black box of some kind. I couldn't see my body but I could feel my fists as I pounded violently on the cold, black walls around me. I kept screaming that I wasn't dead yet and for someone to please let me out of there. With another swishing sound, I found myself being lifted off the table and on to the stretcher. I couldn't breathe, but I couldn't get anyone's attention. Apparently, I had been given some kind of drug that paralyzed me. Frantically, I tried to shake any part of my body in the hope of attracting someone's attention. Finally, I managed to move my legs, ever so slightly. It was then that the doctor looked at me and realized that I was in serious distress. I was heaved back onto the table, where oxygen was forced into my lungs and I felt the oxygen flow in. I practically gulped it down in relief.

I had been awake for nearly the whole operation. I assume they tried to give me as little anesthesia as possible, for the baby's sake, but this was a little bit much! I told the doctor later that I could feel him cut me and that it felt like a burning pinch and pull. He seemed a little surprised that I knew that. (Believe me, I would rather not have known!) Then I told him that he and someone else had been talking about sailboats, before all the rushing and screaming began. Again, he looked surprised. But when I told him about hearing them screaming at me, being trapped in a black box, begging to be set free, insisting that I wasn't dead yet, he looked at me like I was nuts and ordered me an anti-depressant tablet! It's no wonder that most people never tell their doctors about these kinds of experiences! No one ever told me why, when I received my bill for the hospital stay, that I had been charged for two emergency resuscitations during the delivery.

After my close call with death, I have come to believe that I must be here for a good reason or else I would have left that day. I wasn't allowed to leave. I guess God knew if that if I had gotten so much as a glimpse of that light, I'd have followed it and never looked back.

My baby and I had less than a 50/50 chance when we entered the delivery room. I remember, at one point, while praying, I promised God that if he would let me and my baby live, I would teach my baby about the kind and loving God that I knew. I must have said something right, because seven days later my son and I went home. God kept his end of the bargain and I've kept mine, too.

It truly would seem that death is only a change in a life—not the end of a life. With this in mind, many of the things I used to worry about no longer seem so important to me. My priorities have changed. I see the bigger picture now. You've probably heard the expression, "She can't see the forest for the trees." Well, I don't just see the forest, any more. I see the whole planet.

On September 1, 1990, I had the most incredible dream of my life. I told everyone whom I knew about it; even a few strangers. I told an Episcopal priest about it and she told me that God had spoken to me, and that I was blessed. I told some of my Native American friends about it and they called it my medicine dream. They told me that the Hummingbird was my totem and that this was a pretty cool totem to have.

Here is my medicine dream...

I was sitting in a lawn chair in my parents' back yard—right where *the mark* in the yard was, right in the middle of the circle. My children were playing in the yard as I watched. I enjoyed hearing their laughing voices and feeling the sunshine on my face. All of a sudden, I heard this loud buzzing noise, whizzing around my head. Instinctively, I picked up the little whiffleball bat that was lying on the ground next to my chair and I began swatting at the small, dark thing that was now flying around my face. I assumed it was a bumblebee and that it was going to sting me. I hit the thing and it fell to my feet. As I leaned down to get a better look, I was horrified to see that what I had struck down wasn't a bumblebee at all. It was a tiny, precious hummingbird. As it lay there, trembling, I scooped it up into my hands and began to cry. At that very moment, I wished that I had been the one who had been struck down. I cried out to the sky, "God, please don't let this poor creature pay for *my* lesson with *his* life. Take mine instead." At that instant, the world changed. The familiar sunlight took on an unusual quality. Shadows changed and sound stopped. I could no longer hear the voices of my children, nor could I see them. It was as if the whole world, and time itself, came to a screeching halt. Then, from all around me, I could hear a gentle male voice, speaking softly. He said, "Do you understand this?" I shouted to the sky, "YES! I struck out at this poor creature before I even knew what he was. I judged much too quickly. I could easily have gotten up and walked away. Instead, I chose to strike out at something I didn't understand. Please forgive me and please don't let this innocent life pay for my lesson learned. I will never forget this!" Then, I heard the voice say, "Very good." The next thing I knew, the world and time were returned to normal, and the tiny hummingbird, cupped in my hands, was coming around nicely. I took him inside the house, nursed him back to health and he stayed in our house for the whole winter. He stuck to me like glue and followed me everywhere. The following summer (this was a very long dream!), I set him free and we never saw him again.

This was to be the first of my many "virtual reality" dreams. Maybe I did speak to God that night in my dream. If so, he taught me a powerful lesson that applies to many aspects of life, including extraordinary, anomalous experiences. Maybe it's not such a bad lesson for us all to learn.

ELEVEN

The Future

~

Please keep an open mind and an open heart when you read this chapter. It contains my thoughts and feelings about what the future may hold for me—and for the human race. At this point in the game, none of us can really have much more than feelings, intuitions, and educated guesses.

I hate predictions. I try not to make them. If I do make public my feelings about the future, I try to reiterate that these are merely my *feelings* and they may mean absolutely nothing. On a personal level, I believe there are several paths that we can follow and that our fate is determined by our choices. But I also believe that divine guidance is available to us—within us—should we ever decide to ask for it and to truly hear it when it is offered. As for the bigger picture, I was raised to believe that there is a reason why "big" events must happen, even though we might not understand the reason at the time. And little things happen so that something bigger can happen later.

Most of the predictions I've heard from others in the past simply did not come true. On those rare occasions when someone hits it right on the mark, I figure that the someone in question either got very lucky or that they must be very special—gifted. I doubt I am such a someone. It does occur to me, however, that I am somewhat more sensitive to impending changes in the world. Animals are often aware of impending earthquakes due to changes in the electromagnetic fields that surround the planet. You may even have seen your family dog anxiously seeking shelter under the couch before a big storm hits. They can sense it coming before we do. This might be what's happening to me. My awareness of my surroundings has heightened to the extent that sometimes I sense things before most other people catch on. Perhaps this is what happens to us as a result of our experiences and that's why so many experiencers tend to make a lot of predictions. An overabundance of inner-awareness spills over into the physical realm in which we live, and we become supersensitive to that, also. It makes me wonder if something isn't being awakened within us—something in all of us, long-lost, that is now being found again. I see it as an awareness of the planet we live on and the connection we have to it, to each other, and to all that is life: God, or whatever name you choose to call *It*.

I feel as though I'm beginning to remember another world, another existence. My older sister and I both have, at various times in our lives and independently of one another, made the statement that if one of us were ever to fall ill with some catastrophic disease, we would know exactly what to do. We both feel that we had been told to go alone to find an open field, to lie down in it, go to sleep, and, the next morning, when we awake, we would be healed. Neither one of us had ever mentioned this to the other. It only came to light through Budd's separate questioning of us during his investigations.

~

I used to have a reoccurring dream; it started when I was very young. In the dream, I was lying in a ditch, covered by fallen trees, hiding from violence all around me. The sky was a funny color—a very dark, ominous purple-blue mix. Blue and red streaks of light flashed back and forth across this frightening sky. The wind was ferocious and rain was falling so hard that it blew horizontal across the open field in front of me and stung my face as it hit me. A large hill stood in front of me, perhaps seventy-five feet from where I was lying. I was trying desperately to reach it. I crawled on my belly toward the hill, digging my fingers into the dirt as I dragged myself across the ground so as not to be blown away by the terrible wind. The noise all around me was deafening. I felt pure panic. My only hope seemed to be making it to that hill. As I finally reached the base of the hill and was able to look up, I could see a man standing at the very top. He was dressed all in white; he was dry and pristine—the wind seemed to have no effect on him. He was very beautiful, with golden hair draped around his shoulders. His eyes were bright blue, radiating pure love and calmness. When he spoke to me, it was as if he spoke directly to my heart and my mind. He said, "It's time to go. You are safe, now." Suddenly, the most incredible feeling of relief and calm swept over me and then the dream would end.

During a visit to Cahokia Mounds in Illinois, built by Indians hundreds of years ago, I *found* the hill *and* the trees *and* the ditch that I had dreamed about before so many times in my life. I can't describe to you the feeling I had when I stood atop that hill (a mound) and looked back at the ditch and trees. It was a combination of peace and relief, with an uncomfortable twinge of anxiety. I don't know what it all means, but if ever I find myself in a situation similar to the one in my dream, I'll know where to go.

~

My sister and I both have said for many years, independently, on multiple occasions, that the world would be a very different place by the beginning of the 21st Century. But it would be only for the young and the strong. I didn't know what that meant, exactly, but I knew that I would be a part of it; and my sister she knew that she would be, too. I do know that no one need be lost in the changes. If they are, it will be their choice.

I always felt that some of the changes would be real, physical ones— that things would happen to change the whole look of the planet. I felt that extreme governmental and social changes would occur, and that these would act as triggers for me, to help me to remember what I am supposed to do next.

I felt as though the whole world—all of humanity—would soon be embarking on the greatest journey of all. As time passes, I think this will become increasingly obvious to everybody. We are beginning to experience some profound changes as a species. I feel that part of why I am here is to help open as many hearts and minds as I can, so that these changes will come as easily as possible for those who are still bound by fear. The only way I know how to describe the changes that I feel are coming is to say that the human race is about to take the final step on the evolutionary ladder. This change will not be a physical one; we won't lose our pinkies or our appendix. We will lose our fear: our sense of separation and individuality. We will learn how to escape the confinements of our linear-time minds and realize our potential as "one." The veils of our minds will finally part and we will remember what we really are, and why we are here.

I can't really explain to you why I think "aliens" have something to do with this. I only know that they do. Perhaps they are simply another manifestation of the Life of which we are all a part and they are helping us to remember, to evolve, so that they can evolve, also. I believe that all life is somehow connected. This includes "them," too. Maybe, in helping us, they are helping themselves. Maybe it is more than just ourselves that we are holding back through our fear, through our desire for control and our lack of responsibility. Maybe they're getting tired of waiting on us, and our encounters with them are subtle (or perhaps not-so-subtle!) reminders of the role we have to play as a species.

I believe that the answers we spend a lifetime seeking have been within us all along. We waste so much time searching outside of ourselves that we miss the whole point—we forget to look within, to the source of all true love, growth, and oneness.

There's so much in my mind and heart that I want to share with you, but for which I haven't the words to adequately express. I think you have to feel it, rather than hear it. I wish I could climb inside each and every one of you and make you *know*, but I can't. You'll have to arrive at your own realizations for them to have any real meaning for you. All I can do is plant the seed and hope that it grows.

I am amazed at the things that I find myself feeling and thinking. To think where I came from, to where I am now and where I might be heading, seems incredible to me. I feel I'm living proof of a larger plan. In a way, sharing it with others feels kind of weird and embarrassing. I feel naked right now. I realize that I still have much to learn. My own process of change and growth has only just begun.

I think it is safe to say at least part of that "prediction" is coming true right now. Starting with 9/11 and now with the pandemic, we are seeing in real time how life is changing. Eventually, we will change how we think about money, about daily life, about each other. It will change *all* our priorities and how we think about religion, spirituality, *how we think about ourselves. Nothing* will ever be the same. Old rules will become meaningless. Money will be worthless. Time and skill will become the currency of choice. Now, that isn't to say that it will be all bad. And I think we may have done this "reboot" a few times in the distant past. But for some who can't adapt to changing situations, who refuse to even consider things that don't fit into their paradigm, it won't be an easy transition. But this is the only way humans are going to survive on this planet. We cannot survive if we continue on our current path.

It doesn't take a psychic (or an experiencer) to know that the world is headed in a dangerous direction right now. I sometimes entertain the idea that the Large Hadron Collider must have ripped a hole in the space-time continuum and some shitty alternative reality is now seeping into ours, like some drippy, leaky trash bag. Obviously, I have no idea what is happening, but I know it's not good. And, in a world where you aren't sure whom or what to trust anymore, it is *supremely* important that you learn to trust *yourself*, your instincts, your power. Your gut will never lead you astray, and the more you trust it, the better it gets.

I believe we have the power to change our reality. *Nothing* is written in stone. The changes we are facing can ultimately be blessings in disguise. Not all good things come easy. Anyone who has ever pushed a seven-pound baby out of her body can tell you this.

At the end of the day, I can share with you my thoughts about the future, but they are just going to be my opinions and nothing more. I have come to understand that we need not try to predict the future. We *create* the future.

TWELVE

"Emily"

~

4073 A Pinehurst Dr E 898-6809

12/19/77 vag. discharge. monilial. Rx Moncstat cream

2/23/78 problem with catching and clicking with the R T-M joint. X-ray ordered preg test done which tends to be pos. X-RAY CANCELED

3/2/78 Preg test - neg

3/13/78 in for preg test which was neg, two wks ago it was pos. will ordered another one at the hosp, most likely she is

5/5/78 in with cramping in the morn and after intercourse at nite. Has tenderness in the uterus. Has mild infection. Started on Vibramycin and Bentyl 22

5/8/78 R Monastat, Mylanta & Cl. tips. Stop Bentyl

5/9/78 diarrhea c Her colitis is acting up. Rx ProBanthine and if no imp, will use Lomotil

9/19/78 having abd cramping , pain, colitis. No rel. with ProBanthine before, just gradually got better on diet. Will try Bentyl 20mgs

10/2/78 pneumonia; seen at the hosp . Still coughing immensley. Placed on urgent list for adm. to CHI. Cont on Keflex given to her at hosp. then will switch to KIE in the meantime

10-19-79 ?TM Hemrsh. pneum.

11/2/78 still having cough and no temp; productive of white sputum. Sent lab for cult, chest x-ray and legioniers titer. Given Rx Minocin 50mgs q.i.d. and Quadrinol

11/24/78 Urine neg Preg test neg B/P 140/82

12/5/78 Preg test Pos Referred to Dr. McCrue

7/31/79 B/P 140/90

7/31/79 UTI; Rx Bactrim one b.i.d.

8/2/79 in for reaction to Bactrim; is having a rash and swelling. Rx Tetracycline today 500mgs q.i.d. Will d.c. Bactrim. Given Lasix for swelling.

9/10/79 120/80

9/10/79 in for h.a. and B/P doing well. Started on Micrainin as needed for h.a.

11/13/79 R slow K 2 brd

12-11-79 Lamet___

12/18/79 Is having problems with "flip-flopping of her heart". I can't tell whether it's a tachycardia or just palpitations. Was ck'd by Dr. Decatur last night and was given an unknown injection which knocked her out. Exam today is normal. Rx Valium 2mg t.i.d. Advised to count her pulse when this occurs and to report back if medication doesn't help.

This part of my story—the possibility that I have a missing daughter—is the most difficult to talk about, for a number of reasons. The most obvious reason is that it's the strangest part of the whole abduction phenomenon and the hardest for people to believe. It's also embarrassingly painful for me to recall. In addition to the high strangeness of it, I have also to deal with all the normal emotions a woman has when she loses a baby—the feelings of inadequacy, the loss, the longing. I still feel them, strongly. Even now, I feel a knot in my stomach when I think about it. It's something I'll never forget—and I'll never stop feeling.

I have a really hard time believing that it was a hysterical pregnancy. I am under the assumption that women who have hysterical pregnancies desperately want a baby. I definitely *didn't* want to become pregnant at the time. Born in 1959, I was barely eighteen years old! I wanted to have children someday, but not then. My boyfriend and I had gotten engaged in December 1977, decided to marry the following June, and were looking forward to having some time alone together before we started a family. When I actually heard my doctor speak the words, "You're pregnant," my first reaction was "Oh, man, no, not yet!"

~

I must backtrack a little here to tell of a strange experience I had with a couple of girl friends in November of 1977; it's an integral part of the story of my life. About 2:00am, Dorothy, Roberta and I were driving around on the country roads of rural Indiana. I was supposed to be spending the night with Dorothy and she was supposed to be spending the night with me. I'm sure that's not the first time that teenagers have used this excuse to gain some freedom. It's a classic. We really didn't have anything to do, but the thought that we were "free"—that we were actually doing something we really weren't supposed to be doing because we were still considered as children by our parents—it gave us a "charge." I guess it made us feel more like adults, even though, in retrospect, it was actually kind of stupid. When you're eighteen, you think you know it all.

There was nothing else three teenage girls could legally do at two in the morning. We were basically "good" kids. Besides, we were on a "mission." We were going to spy on Dorothy's boyfriend. He lived in an old farmhouse, and we were going to see if he was where he said he was going to be. We figured he might also be using the "I'm spending the night with her/him" excuse.

While driving north on a dark, deserted country road, I noticed a bright, white flashing light in the sky. It was moving toward us from the east. At first, it seemed pretty steady and I assumed it was an airplane. Teasing my friends, I said, "Hey! Look, you guys. It's a UFO!" (Don't ask me why I said that, because I have no idea!) Dorothy and I started to giggle as Roberta jumped up from behind me to get a better look at it. The startled look on her face was priceless. We had been watching the light for a minute or two when suddenly it started to flash really brightly, dancing all over the sky. It was a beautiful but startling sight.

Dorothy and I were fascinated—almost mesmerized—by it, although I also felt myself becoming a little anxious. Roberta, on the other hand, became *very* upset. She dove behind my seat, curled up on the floorboard in the fetal position and began to whine: "Come on you guys, let's get out of here! I'm getting scared!" I looked over at Dorothy with an ornery grin on my face and then turned around in my seat to look at Roberta. I was quite amused to see her lying there with her coat over her head.

When Dorothy slowed the car to get a better look at the light, it suddenly shot almost directly overhead. Dorothy and I shouted, almost simultaneously, "*Wow*! Check this out!" I could feel the blood rush to my face as my heart began to pound with a mix of anxiety and excitement. Roberta went ballistic and began screaming at us to "get the hell outta here, right now!" Dorothy and I looked at each other and started giggling, hysterically. The odd light was creeping us out, but it didn't bother us as much as Roberta's reaction did. We were nervous about the whole situation and when teenage girls get nervous, they giggle.

That was the last conscious memory I had of that night. The next thing I remembered, we were driving back into town, feeling kind of dazed and disoriented, when Dorothy looked at her watch. She seemed surprised at the fact that it was now 4:30am. She said something like, "Time sure flies when you're having fun!" Yet, there was a hint of sarcasm in her voice.

I had nightmares about that night for years afterward. None of them made much sense and I quickly tried to forget the details as soon as I woke up. I had vague dreams of feeling chased and hunted, like a wild animal, and I always seemed to wake up just before I could get a good look at my attacker's face. I remembered dreaming about pain—lots of pain.

When Budd began investigating my family's experiences, I underwent hypnosis to recall details of that particular night. I remembered seeing the light in the sky and snickering at Roberta for being such a chicken.

I remembered the car stopping and seeing a bright flash of light in the car, as if someone inside had taken a flash picture. Then, I saw a big, black craft, racing toward the car from directly in front of us. The whole car was enveloped in a black cloud. I remembered being pulled from the vehicle—legs first—by some unseen force, and then finding myself in a white room with strange looking balconies and railings. I remembered feeling naked and cold, lying helplessly on a very hard, narrow, elevated surface. I couldn't see it but I figured it was a table of some kind. I remembered feeling a tremendous pressure on my abdomen, right above my pubic bone, and feeling as if I would explode. Then, I felt the same kind of pressure under my right breast and heard an extremely loud sucking sound, like when you're drinking a milk shake with a straw and get to the bottom of the glass. Finally, I heard someone tell me, in my head: "It's over." I just lay there, my legs propped up. As the entity leaned over me from above my head, I could see the grey face that I have seen so many times since. Then, those huge, black eyes looked deeply into mine and told me to rest.

The next thing I remembered, I was back in the car. I could see stars and sky out of the window, but the inside of the car was black. I could feel my hand on the door handle but I couldn't see it. I could feel the seat under me. I wanted to get out and run, but I couldn't. I couldn't move. I couldn't see anything inside the car and I couldn't hear anything, not even my own breathing. Somehow, I knew Dorothy was no longer in the car with me. I panicked and wondered if they were doing to her the same thing they had done to me. I wanted to help her but I couldn't and I somehow felt responsible for what I thought was happening to her in those moments. I felt guilty for teasing Roberta about being chicken. I wanted to cry, but I couldn't even do that.

Suddenly the blackness was gone and I could see Dorothy standing outside in front of the car, looking up at something unseen. I could move again, and I could hear Roberta whimpering from the back seat. Quickly forgetting everything that had just happened, I jumped out of the car and walked over to Dorothy. We both stood there for a short time just looking up at the clear, starry night. I asked her if she could still see the light. She told me, "No, they're gone now." I remember looking at her kind of funny, thinking, "What's this 'they' stuff?" Then, our eyes met. I didn't have to verbalize my question. It was as if, for one brief moment, we both realized what had just happened, and then, just as quickly, forgot all about it. We walked slowly and silently back to the car. We got in, we told Roberta it was gone, and we drove off.

Budd interviewed Dorothy when he came to our house during the investigation. When we arrived at her apartment that night, we told her about June 30, 1983, and about Budd's investigation. Budd asked Dorothy about that night in November and the light we had seen. She piped up: "Which light are you talking about, the light in the sky or the light on the ground?" Her comments took me by surprise because I hadn't remembered the light being on the ground.

She said that she remembered getting out of the car to look at the light on the ground. She didn't remember much after that except for remarking at how the time had flown by. She did not want to undergo hypnosis; the thought of it made her very nervous. It made her stomach hurt. She really didn't want to remember anything about that night. I can't say that I blame her!

Funny thing about this whole affair—after Budd interviewed her, Dorothy and I kind of drifted apart. I got the distinct impression that being with me was triggering a memory in her that made her very uncomfortable. Whenever our eyes met, I could see the pain in her. And I recognized it all too well.

We did run into each other several years later. She told me after I had brought Budd to meet her that she could not stop thinking about that night in November and the light on the ground. I have often wondered if this incident in November, 1977, was actually the night I got pregnant and *not* the night in December, when my boyfriend "Eddie" had asked me to marry him and we had sex for the first time. I guess no one will really ever know. For sanity sake, I have always assumed that my first pregnancy was my boyfriend's baby, and I suppose I always will. I really detest seeing headlines in the tabloids that read, "I Had an Alien's Baby!" and certainly I would never want my experience to be put in the same category with these ridiculous stories.

I had a light period in January of '78. Despite this, I felt I was pregnant (as it turned out, I had periods for the first couple of months with my two sons' pregnancies, and I was later told that this is not at all uncommon in some women). I had all the symptoms of pregnancy. Nausea in the morning (and sometimes evening, too), tender breasts, fatigue, more frequent urination and—a curious one— gagging whenever I brushed my teeth (I also experienced this during my other two pregnancies). My friends kept telling me, "Girl, you're pregnant!" I kept saying, "No way!" When you're pregnant, live in the Midwest, have a daddy like mine, are barely eighteen and are not married, you'd better make *damn sure* you're pregnant before you go telling your father about it. No one would want to incur the wrath of Daddy without good cause!

By mid-February, my period was late. I talked to my mother about it and she took me to our family doctor. He gave me the standard pregnancy tests and pelvic exam and told me I was, indeed, pregnant. If I recall correctly, there was even some debate as to how far along I was. He felt I was farther along than I did. I was counting back from the night in December when my boyfriend proposed to me. Except for remembering the light in the sky, all conscious memory of the experience in November had slipped into the shadows of my mind.

Everything seemed normal and, as the days passed, I began to accept the fact that I was going to have a baby and I began to look forward to sharing a child with my soon-to-be-husband. We decided to move the wedding date from June to April, so that I wouldn't look so pregnant. One weekend in mid-March, I had gone to my sister "Laura's" house to babysit her kids so that she and her husband could have some time off. I figured it would be good practice for me since I would have a child of my own soon. Besides, I had always been the free babysitter in the family.

After I had put the kids to bed for the night, I went into my sister's bedroom to watch TV and talk on the phone with my fiancé. While I was talking to Eddie, I started to get the feeling that someone was looking at me through the bedroom window. I couldn't see anything, but I sure could feel it! I cut off Eddie quickly, without telling him how I was feeling, and moved into the living room after we hung up.

As soon as I left the bedroom, the feeling went away. I dismissed my anxiety as "pregnancy nerves" and eventually I shook it off. I lay down on the couch to watch *The Bob Newhart Show*, one of my favorites. After a while, I grew sleepy and decided to roll over to get more comfortable. I figured I could "listen" to my show just as well as look at it (that was always one of Mom's favorite excuses for falling asleep on the couch in front of the TV).

As I lay with my back to the TV and my face stuffed into the pillow, I began to feel someone gently stroking my back, my shoulders, and the side of my face. I was startled at first but, almost instantaneously, a thought popped into my head: *It's just one of the kids.* A lovely feeling of peace and warmth washed over me. I quickly relaxed and let the soothing strokes lull me to sleep.

Years later, partly under hypnosis and partly on my own, I remembered the rest of the story. I remembered being on a strange table. It seemed to be in sections and the bottom dropped out of it while the legs began to elevate. I was somehow stuck to this table and it pulled my legs so far apart I felt as if I was going to be ripped in half. Then I could feel something large and cold going into my vagina and I felt as if I were being opened up inside like a pupil dilates. I could feel my pelvic bones. They felt as if they were being pulled apart, strained to the limit. I felt like a wishbone! Suddenly, I felt as if my abdomen was being sucked flat from the inside out. I could feel the pain and wanted to scream out but I couldn't. Then I saw her.

She was being held by the grey, black-eyed entity. His hands were cupped and I could see something moving around in them. At first, I didn't realize what it was. She was so tiny! As soon as I realized what had happened, I screamed—in my mind, I think, not with my mouth, but he heard it anyway. I screamed, "It's not fair! It's mine! I hate you! I hate you! It's not fair!" You son-of-a-bitch, you bastard!" I felt he was actually taken aback by my reaction to the whole thing and took measures to quiet me down immediately. That's all I could remember. I think I may have actually passed out after that because, to this day, I can't remember anything else.

The next morning, I awoke in my little niece's bed. I had no memory of how I had got gotten there. The very first thing on my mind was, "How in the hell did I get in here?" The second thing I thought was, "Oh my God! I'm not pregnant anymore! My little girl is gone!" I looked all over the bed for signs of a miscarriage. Then, I got up, went to the bathroom, and checked myself. I could find nothing, not a sign of a miscarriage anywhere. I couldn't figure out why I felt like I was no longer pregnant. At that point, I had no conscious memory of the previous night. I was panic-stricken and I felt really stupid. How could I explain this panic? What in the hell was wrong with me?

I called Mom from "Laura's" house and told her that I thought I was having a period and needed to see the doctor right away. I was actually spotting lightly but I didn't know how to explain it or justify why I wanted to go to the doctor. I needed confirmation that I was still pregnant for my own peace of mind. Mom called the doctor, who told her to tell me to not be alarmed, just put my feet up for a while and if it got worse or I experienced pain, to call him back.

Well, that didn't satisfy me. I called my friend, Dorothy, and told her how I was feeling. She told me that she was going to Planned Parenthood the following Monday to get some birth control and she suggested that I go in with her. She said I should I tell them that I wanted a pregnancy test and not to tell them I had already seen my doctor and had been confirmed pregnant. That way I would get a positive result and I'd feel better. Plus, it wouldn't cost me anything, I wouldn't have to tell anyone how I felt, and I wouldn't have to explain why I wanted another test. I thought it was a great idea, so, on Monday morning, Dorothy picked me up, and then, along with Roberta, off we went to the Planned Parenthood clinic.

I proceeded as planned. The nurse called me back to the exam room. She informed me that my test was negative and that, if I didn't start my period within the week, I should return to the clinic or talk to my family doctor.

I went into shock. Tears streamed down my face as we drove home. I sobbed, uncontrollably, "They took my baby! That was *my* baby!" I'm sure my friends didn't have the slightest idea how to respond to me, but they didn't question what I was saying.

Dorothy dropped me off at my sister's house, and from there I called Mom again. I told her she had to take me to the doctor because something was terribly wrong. I couldn't tell her what because I didn't understand it myself, but she heard me crying and must have thought I was in pain. She picked me up right away and, on March 13, 1978, we went to the doctor's office.

When we got there, I told them I'd had what seemed to be a period and that I'd had another test, which turned out to be negative. They looked at me as if I were nuts; nonetheless, they gave me yet another test. It was negative. They took me to a room and set me up for another pelvic exam.

The doctor was very quiet throughout. When he was done, he motioned for me to get dressed and told me to meet him in the office and to bring my mother with me.

I remember the look on his face as Mom and I sat there. It was obvious that he was as confused and concerned as I was. Then, he said to me, "I'm not quite sure what went on here, but you are not pregnant. I see nothing out of the ordinary. You look healthy, completely normal. Sometimes, these things happen and we can't explain them. You're young and healthy. You'll have more children someday."

As I sat there, quietly crying, he told me, "I think the best thing for all of us to do is to just forget this ever happened." I said to him, "Oh, I'll never forget this, as long as I live!" My mother asked him if I would need a D&C since I had been pregnant and now wasn't. He said that he didn't think there was anything to clean out, that I felt normal size and looked just fine, but if I should start having problems, I should come back. He mentioned something about sending me to the hospital for another pregnancy test before he did the pelvic exam, but afterward decided not to. The car ride home was quiet. We would never talk about that day again.

After the incident of June 30, 1983, I began to think of that first pregnancy again. I cannot explain why looking at the mark in my parents' back yard would trigger memories of this lost pregnancy, but I think that fact is significant in itself. Even though I didn't consciously think about that part of my life much, I had never forgotten it. I had been able to control my feelings and keep how I felt about it to myself for many years. I never talked about it with anyone, except Dorothy. After Dorothy and I drifted apart, I was alone with my memories of that time in my life. And that was okay with me until that night in June.

During one of Budd's trips to Indianapolis to interview some of our family and friends, I told him about the missing pregnancy. I really don't know what possessed me to tell him about her.

We had been at a nice little restaurant having lunch. On the way back to Mom and Dad's house I began to think about the baby again. We pulled up in the driveway and, as Budd started to get out of the car, I just sat there. Budd sensed there was something on my mind and began to question me about it. That's when I blurted out the fact that I had lost a baby when I was eighteen. As soon as I realized what I had said, I felt like such an idiot! I felt so sorry for him at that moment. The look on his face said, "Well, I'm really sorry to hear about that but, what the hell does that have to do with anything?" Then, I thought to myself, "Jesus H. Christ! What have I done?" I told him I had no idea why I felt I had to tell him about the baby, except, for some reason, I believed there was a connection between my lost baby and whatever happened in my parents' back yard that night in June of 1983.

I'm not really sure exactly what Budd thought that day. I do know that after he had time to think about it and began to hear of more cases very similar to mine, things started to fall into place for him. Eventually, I told Budd about seeing my baby again, a few years after losing her.

I've had a few "dreams" about seeing my daughter over the years. The "presentation" in Budd's 1987 book, *Intruders*, was the most dramatic. That "presentation" was also depicted in the mini-series of the same name that aired on CBS in May of 1992.

On October 3, 1983, "they" showed my daughter to me, and "they" allowed me to remember. Because I couldn't take her with me, and because my emotional connection to her was so very strong, I believe that someone—the entity I always seemed to recognize—felt sorry for me. By their allowing me to remember this presentation, I could take some of her with me. That's my feeling, anyway.

This was the "dream" that I remembered:

I had been sitting on a table in a white room. I felt as if a lot more had happened earlier that night but this was the only part I could remember without hypnosis. To this day, I never have remembered how this particular incident began. It was very large room. The grey, whom I always seemed to recognize, helped me off the table and stood next to me as more grey entities came into the room. I knew something was up, but I didn't know what. This had never happened before. I felt some kind of electricity—a sense of excitement—in the air. It seemed that they were quite pleased with me, and I remember one of them reaching out to touch my shoulder, almost as a gesture of support. Of course, that was my *interpretation* of the touch. It could have been for some very different reason. Whatever the case, until then, I had never remembered feeling that much emotion from them. As I looked up, a small girl was escorted into the room, flanked by two of the greys. For some reason, I felt these two greys were female. Outwardly, they didn't look any different from the rest, but something about their eyes and the way they "felt" made me think they were female. The little girl was about the height of a four-year-old child, but she seemed very fragile. She had tiny ears, set low on her head, a tiny mouth and large, blue eyes. Her forehead was very large and her body seemed very thin and frail. She had snow-white hair that was patchy on her large head, and her complexion was very pale. I remembered thinking how strange she looked when she blinked. Her eyeballs rolled back and her eyelids met in the middle of her eyes. Nevertheless, I thought she was absolutely beautiful! I was in love and my maternal instincts overwhelmed me very quickly. She looked like an angel and my first instinct was to run up to her, to grab her and hold her. It was almost as if she read my mind because, no sooner had thought crossed my mind than she jumped and tried to hide behind one of the two entities holding her hands. My heart sank as she did so. It was then that I realized that she was just as afraid of me as I had been of the greys. It was obvious that the mere sight of me frightened her.

Looking back, I could see how I huge and scary I must have appeared to her if all she had ever known were the little grey guys. At the time, though, all I could feel was crushed. I decided not to go to her, so as not to frighten her even more. I remembered how I had felt when I was younger and I thought the greys were going to touch me. But holding myself back was so hard to do. As soon as I had the thought that I would not grab her, I could have sworn I saw her crack a tiny, timid half smile as she peeked at me from behind the entity. It was the sweetest thing I had ever seen and my heart felt as if it would burst! The grey standing beside me looked at me and I felt he somehow told me that this was a good thing, and that I had done well and that I should be proud. He didn't quite seem to understand my mixed emotions. He told me many things, most of which I still have not remembered. I do remember him saying something about a father taking care of his children. That is when I asked him if I could please take her home with me. He told me no, that I would be unable feed her. He promised me I would see her again and that I had to leave soon or else I would get sick. He escorted me to a round platform. I stepped up onto it and I turned toward him. He stepped in front of me and took my hands in his. They felt squishy and cool. He looked up into my eyes. Suddenly, I began to feel every human emotion shoot through me like a bullet, all at once. "What the hell's wrong with me!" I thought, "Why am I feeling all these feelings?" It was probably the most intense moment of my life. Suddenly I realized that I wasn't the one having all those feelings. They were coming from *him*. Like some lame attempt at "feeling" for me, of relating to me in my own human terms. He let go of my hands and then the whole room began to look as if I were seeing it through the heat of a fire, real shimmery and wavy. The next thing I remember, I was lying on the grass behind my parents' home. I looked up and could see a craft above me, starting to move away. It looked like a headband with white lights on it. I got up and went to the house, but all the doors were locked. I stood at the back door and called for my mother to let me in. Mom heard me and quickly came to answer my call. She never said one word to me. She just let me in and went back to bed. Mom says she remembers hearing me call her name that night, but she doesn't remember letting me in. I know the entities are famous for deceiving their "subjects," but I choose to believe them when they tell me that I will see her again, someday. I have to believe it. I keep telling myself that people who find out they are adopted almost always seek out their biological parents eventually. I figure if the little girl really is a part of me, then someday she'll feel "the pull." The human part of her will drive her to find me. I can only hope.

~

Many people ask me how I came about naming her "Emily." That's a pseudonym that Budd chose to use in his book. The real name I gave her was Elizabeth.

The entity I have been able to recognize during all my encounters told me that, if it would make me feel better about leaving her with them, I could give her a name and they would use it for her while she was with them. I had always liked the name Elizabeth. Growing up, I had always said if I ever had a little girl, that would be her name. I called various dolls by this name throughout my childhood. It was a name I held close to my heart. It was a name intended for that first child, had she ever been born to me. It was an appropriate name in light of how I felt about the little girl I saw in my "dream" that night. That's how real she is to me.

It is this aspect of the phenomena that is the most emotional, the most embarrassing and the most ridiculed. Can you blame people for not wanting to tell others about something like this? Would you want to open your heart to inevitable ridicule and pain? I didn't want Budd to put anything about the baby in his book. It took considerable convincing on Budd's part for me to finally give in and to let that part of my story be included. I just didn't know if I could handle having to talk about something so bizarre, so unbelievable, and yet so personal and emotional. And I felt it would lower the credibility of the rest of the case. Certainly, I could never expect anyone to believe a word of this! I never would have, had it not happened to me. And I still can't be sure of exactly what happened. I still prefer to refer to "the presentation" as a dream. It's the only rational way I can live with this.

What convinced me to finally reveal the "baby" part of my abduction experiences was the fact that I was not alone. Budd began to hear from many thousands of men and women from all around the world who claimed similar experiences to mine. If ever anyone knew their secret heartache—their confusion and isolation—it was me. I thank God I've had the support of my family and friends. Many of you won't be so fortunate. My prayers are with you, always. If I had been able to tell someone about this earlier without being dismissed as a total nut, perhaps my life would have taken a different course sooner. If I can spare just one person from experiencing what I went through emotionally, then I will be happy to have told my story.

No one will ever know exactly what has happened to me and my family—why I've remembered what I have; why seen the things I've seen. I find it intriguing that hundreds-of-thousands of men and women have exactly the same memories as me. It tells me that *something* is going on. What that something is, we can only speculate. When I hear anyone claim to have all the answers, my red flags go up fast. Hell, I've experienced these phenomena directly, and I still don't know much of anything for sure! There's no denying my feelings and the hard, physical evidence, but as for the rest? One day, perhaps, all will become clear.

THIRTEEN

K.O. and Dave

~

In 1987, Budd Hopkins came to DePauw University to give a talk on UFOs. He had just finished his book, *Intruders*, which was centered around my family's experiences. I had visited the university to hear him talk, along with my sister, Kathy ("Laura"), and my new husband, James. This would be my first indication of how the public would react to this strange subject. It was also a chance for me to see Budd again, although we didn't get to see him as much as we would have liked.

K.O.'s daughter was attending the university at the time. She knew of her father's deep interest in the subject of UFOs and had informed him that Budd would be giving a talk there. K.O. attended that night with his wife. Budd asked my sister and me to stand up and say a few words about what our family had experienced, and K.O. videotaped the whole thing (I look at the tape today and laugh. I was so nervous; you could hear my voice shake as I spoke.) K.O. was fascinated by our story, and by me. The investigator in him wanted to learn more.

As the years passed, I would see him at various MUFON meetings and conferences. As it turned out, we shared mutual friends in Rose and Charlie Rich, and would see each other from time to time at their home. I never thought of K.O. as anything more than a nice, kind of nerdy, really intelligent friend. Besides the fact that we were both married, he was fourteen years older than me and definitely not the type to whom I would have been attracted.

~

It all starts one week after I had become engaged to my second husband, James. I was a junior instructor at the local beauty college. On their lunch hour, my students called a psychic who would give one free reading over the phone. After much begging on their part, I agreed to talk to the guy, but not without quite a nasty little attitude about the whole thing. "What's your name, honey" asked the ancient male voice at the end of the line. "Debbie," I replied, hatefully. "You're psychic, you tell me," I thought. Immediately, he said, "You're going to be married three times." I said, "I don't think so." He repeated himself in the same hateful tone of voice that I was using with him. I then informed him that I had just gotten engaged to number two and that there would be no number three if I had anything to say about it. "Go ahead and marry him. It won't last more than five years," he said (it transpired that James and I would split on our fifth anniversary). He proceeded to tell me that number three would be an older man, someone several years older than me who would satisfy and protect me in the way that I needed. He would give me all I needed so I could do what I had come here to do. I told the old psychic that he was out of his mind, that he needed to get a real job. Then, I hung up on him. I told my mother about the phone call when I got home from work that afternoon and we had a good chuckle. But she never forgot it.

In June of 1992, my husband and I split. This was a hectic time in my life and I was experiencing a multitude of feelings. I was leaning on my friends heavily and I'd spent a lot of time on the phone to one of my best friends, Forest Crawford. We had talked about everything imaginable. I had read some books on the subject of angels; I found it fascinating. Once, Forest remarked to me that if I ever had a question as to the direction of my life, I should just ask the universe—that if I listened really close, I might hear an answer. I thought that was a neat idea.

One night, while driving home from my soon-to-be ex-husband's house, where I had gone to get him to sign some paperwork, I began to think about my conversation with Forest. I had mentioned to him that I was feeling a sense of urgency that I had never felt before. I felt as if I needed to be with someone—someone I already knew—before something wonderful could happen. I had run a mental list of all the eligible men I knew who might be what I was looking for. (K.O. was not even on that list!) As I drove down the dark back roads of the shortcut to Mom's, I remembered what Forest had told me earlier. If I asked, someone would answer.

Thank God it was dark and the road was deserted because I began to talk out loud to myself. I'd have died if anyone had seen me! "Okay," I said, "Forest says you guys will answer my questions, so I've got one for you. Who is it I'm supposed to be with?" I swear on a stack of bibles, I heard—as plain as day—a woman's voice in my car say the name "Carl!" It was as if she were sitting right next to me, yelling in my ear. It startled me so much that I nearly drove off the road! Although it's a nice thought, I never really expected to hear an answer! I don't know what possessed me, but I then began to question that answer! "Carl?" I said, "I don't know anyone named Carl. What is this, some kind of joke? I know it's someone I already know so why are you telling me this name?" Then I remembered I had an uncle named Carl. I said, "Well, I have an uncle named Carl, but he's dead, and I don't think he would count anyway. We're related, you know." Twice more I heard the name Carl, each time more insistent than the last. The final time sounded almost as if the woman were getting upset with me for questioning her. I really felt like some kind of nut! When I got home, I told my mother about it and we both laughed, but I still felt kind of weird that I actually *heard* this voice. "Maybe I'm cracking up," I thought. I called my friends, Rose and Forest, and told them about it too. I'm glad I did.

Shortly after my experience with the voice in the car, I was slated to give a talk to a group in Pensacola, Florida. This was August of 1992. K.O. had heard that I was going to go do my talk alone. Knowing the circumstances under which I would be leaving, he thought it would be nice for me to have a familiar face from home there, to lend me moral support. Rather presumptuous and not at all like him, but a nice thought. He had separated from his wife the year before and had taken up traveling as a hobby. Also, being an investigator, he was interested in hearing my talk.

He was somehow able to purchase a ticket on the same flight and in the seat right next to mine, even though my flight had been booked months in advance. He even booked himself a hotel room five minutes away from where I would be staying. I was surprised to find out he had made all these plans before consulting me, but I was truly flattered that he thought that much of me. We were at Rose and Charlie's house the night he told me that he had made arrangements to join me on my trip.

At one point, I looked at him and said, "Hell, K.O., here I am, about to travel with you, and I don't even know your real name. What does K.O. stand for, anyway?" He looked over at me and flashed a big smile: "Karl Osbourn." Immediately, I remembered the voice in the car and the name the voice had told me. I looked at my friend, Rose, who had apparently also remembered what I'd told her. She had this great big grin on her face! I was thinking to myself, "Oh, my God! No! This can't be! What is this, some kind of joke?" Fortunately, my thoughts were known only to Rose.

I know this sounds terrible, but he was one of the last men I would have chosen for myself. It's not that he's not a good guy. It's just he didn't fit my ideal man profile. As it turned out, he couldn't have been a better choice for me, even if it wasn't me doing the choosing! It didn't take me long to realize that I had made some pretty crummy choices in my life up to that point. If I wanted things to change, I figured I had better change my choices.

The day after K.O. and I returned home from our trip to Florida, I began to feel guilty. I had treated him so poorly during the whole trip that I was ashamed of myself. All the time we were down there he was as attentive and protective as he could be. I fought back in my own mind. How dare someone or something force me to be with this man! I didn't like the thought that I had no choice in the whole affair. All my friends commented on how much he appeared to care for me. Vicki, a really good friend, even said to me, "Girlfriend, that boy's in love with you! If my husband can see it, anyone can!" I told her to shut up and not let anyone hear her say that! From day one of that trip, I was, quite frankly, a bitch. The second day after we returned, it was as if a light came on in my head and I could hear that woman's voice again—this time in my head. She said, "Do you really want to push away the best thing that's ever happened to you? This is it, girl. This is what we've been waiting for." I phoned K.O. and apologized for my horrible behavior. The first thing he said in response was, "You know, something told me to give you a little space, that you'd come around." Two days later, I started writing the original edition of this book, which was titled *Abduction! The True Story of Intruders Continues.*

After K.O. and I had dated for a while, we began talking about getting married someday. My mother then reminded me about what the old psychic had told me on the phone that day, several years earlier. That pretty much cinched it for me.

K.O. had been instrumental in the writing of *Abducted!* He got me my first dinosaur computer and taught me how to use it. Before him,

I couldn't even turn one on! He supported me emotionally, spiritually and financially. He helped me to find the confidence to do what I feel I have to do. He taught me to believe that I could document the contents of my heart and mind, and that doing so might help others in the process. I loved him very much and I thanked God every day for my blessings.

I lost my husband, K.O. in 1994, *just* as our book was being published. He committed suicide and, unfortunately, I was a witness to it. It was traumatic and devastating for me and my boys. We loved him very much. But now that time has passed, it seems almost a blessing that I had to see it and that I survived it. He (and God) chose me to be there in his time of need. In his last minutes on earth he heard me tell him that I loved him. He didn't die alone. And it showed me just how strong I truly am. If I can get through that and come out stronger and even more spiritual, then I can overcome and rise above anything. I believe the level with which we can attain spiritual enlightenment is directly related to the experiences we have in this life. Around 18 months later, I remarried.

～

After K.O. passed, I kind of withdrew from everything for a while. And, strangely enough, after an entire lifetime of screwing with me in one way or another, the phenomena let me be. I was never really quite sure why; but I was grateful for it. I needed to go inside myself and find qualities I never believed I possessed: strength and wisdom. I had a big job ahead of me. I had to pull myself together and raise my two sons. And I did. I did better than I ever believed I could.

I got myself back together and carried on. I knew the phenomenon was still there. I could sometimes almost feel it watching, waiting. Somehow, I knew I was supposed to go through this. This time in my life was to be essential for what would lie ahead. Believe it or not, I actually remember having thoughts throughout my life of events that were yet to happen. I remember thinking that I needed to feel this or that—that it would be important later.

It was 10 years after K.O.'s death, at least, before I re-entered the UFO community. It's not that I wasn't interested; it was just that I needed to stay focused on my kids. I still kept a journal of my thoughts and feelings, but the strange phenomena that for years had plagued me and my family seemed to lie dormant, waiting for me to be ready. And, when I was, it was right there to suck me back into the vortex!

K.O. committed suicide on May 16, 1993 while I and every Sheriff and S.W.A.T. team member in Howard County stood by helplessly and watched. We tried to stop him but he was having none of it. He was bound and determined to leave this world. But, before he did, he had promised me that I would be taken care of. I had assumed he was just saying that kind of stuff because he was 15 years older than me. I had no idea what he was actually thinking.

He had said things like, "I'm going to make sure you are taken care of after I'm gone. I will even send you a new husband." I would just look at him and say, "Dude, please. I don't want another husband. I have one." He even mentioned a fellow that was working with him in the Lab at work—a Tech who was very bright. "An up and comer in engineering," he would describe the man who would eventually become my next husband. He even mentioned a parody song this guy had written about K.O. It was written to the tune of *The Banana Boat Song*: "K.O. KAYAYAY.O. K.O, come to work but he want to go home." Cute. He even said to me, "Maybe one day you'll meet him." I didn't give any of it much thought.

The night he died, I was devastated. I had never lost anyone so close to me, let alone *watch* them die. I told the police that the angels had covered my ears and prevented me from hearing the gunshot blast. I honestly didn't remember hearing or seeing anything for several weeks. Even though that was absolutely impossible because I was out there when he did it. I remember seeing a humming bird fly right up to my face within a minute or two after he pulled the trigger. I told the humming bird to go tell him I loved him. And the bird flew to the back yard.

In our state, not just anyone can tell you that someone is officially dead. It has to be a medical doctor/coroner. I followed the ambulance to the hospital ER and from there was rushed into that little room. You know the one where they give you the bad news. By this time some of his family had arrived and were in there with me. Someone came in and said that they needed a family member to identify the body. I couldn't do it. My son in law stepped up and volunteered to do it for me. So, while they were headed to the room where his body was, I was alone. The door opened and in stepped a priest. He wore the collar, and was wearing a name tag and carrying a Bible. He told me he was sorry that my husband had not survived. I remember looking at him and saying to him, "You're a priest. I don't know much about religion, but I have read that if you kill yourself, you will go to hell. He doesn't deserve to go to hell. He was a good man who loved me and I want you to tell me if he is going to hell." The priest was an older man, with white hair and beautiful blue eyes. He knelt at my feet, took my hands in his, and said, "God calls everyone home in different ways. He makes no mistakes. It if wasn't time for him to go, the gun would have misfired, as it often does." He said he would pray for K.O. and me, and he did just that. He made me feel *so much* better. I can't describe to you the feeling of comfort and peace that flooded over me in that moment. And it was in that moment that, somehow, I knew that I was going to be okay.

My boys and I had been staying in a local hotel for several days before K.O. died; he'd been acting increasingly strange, and it scared me. I didn't want my kids to see him like that so we'd been having a "staycation" at a local motel. I would drive them to school in the morning, and then go by the house to try to talk to K.O., feed him, clean up his crazy messes and to encourage him to go get help. I am very fortunate that he didn't take me with him when he left. I never thought about it at the time so I thank God for whatever protected me. I remember going back to the hotel that night because I could *not* stay in that house. The boys went with family. I remember lying on the bed in the hotel. My heart hurt so bad I thought I was going to die. All of a sudden, it felt as if someone lay down beside me on the bed and wrapped their arms around me tight. The warmth that flooded me was so soothing and peaceful it was just like that feeling that swept over me when that priest prayed with me. I quickly drifted off to sleep. I was not one bit scared or even startled, either. I thought it was God.

In the months that followed, I started to remember what I had actually witnessed and it was hard for a long time. But I got through it. K.O. sent me many signs and I experienced a number of strange occurrences.

I had to make the call to friends and relatives. One of the friends, Vicki Lyons, beat me to it. She was a founding member of the Gulf Breeze Research Team and it was her house in which I had a couple of weird nights. K.O. had been on that trip with me, but we were really just friends at that point. K.O. had fallen in love with Vickie's little dogs and spent a lot of time playing with them while he was there.

The morning after K.O. died, Vickie said she was in her laundry room, feeding the dogs, when suddenly she heard K.O.'s voice, "as clear as day" say, 'You know how much I love her, please tell her!'" Now, please realize that Vickie didn't know K.O. was dead yet. I hadn't yet called her. She felt compelled to call me that morning because the feeling that he was there was so strong that she couldn't fight it. When I answered the phone, the first thing I heard was, "Girl, you are gonna think I'm crazy but I gotta tell you this because it was so intense!" I couldn't speak for a minute. When I was finally able to tell her that he had died yesterday, she literally dropped the phone. And when *she* was able to speak, she was crying.

What you don't know about K.O. is that he renovated his whole house for me. He was an Electrical Engineer, amateur astronomer, Ham Radio operator and did OSCAR Moon Bounce in our back yard. He loved the stars and one of the last things we did together was photograph a partial eclipse of the sun. The night he died, a *huge* green Bolide shot across the sky right over our house and was witnessed by dozens of friends from the east side of Indianapolis all the way to Kokomo— and they *all* called me to tell me what they had seen. Even my family, outside smoking that night, all came running in to tell us what they had seen. We all thought about K.O.

A few weeks after K.O.'s death, I was lying on the couch, not feeling good. I had a shitty headache that wouldn't quit, which was not normal for me. All of a sudden, I looked up and, somewhere in the space between the ceiling and me, I could see what looked like a face pushing through an invisible membrane. The face was invisible too, I could see the ceiling behind it, but the shape and details were visible. It kind of reminded me of one of those push-pin toys—you push your hand down on it and the form of your hand pops through the other side. I could see the eyes, the nose, the chin and the cheeks, slowly push into view, right above me. I recognized the face. It was K.O., and he looked worried. I said, out loud, "I'm okay. I promise." With that, it receded back into the membrane and disappeared. That was weird. But in *my* world, it was just another day. And it gets a little weirder still.

It was a few months after his death that I first ventured back out into the public. I was starting to feel alive again. A lot of my friends down in Indianapolis had convinced me to come down and attend a little UFO group meeting. We were just a small group of likeminded people who enjoyed sharing our experiences with one another, watching videos and reviewing books we had read. It was more a social group than anything. We would sometimes attend conferences together, as well. I know they were worried about me and I appreciated the opportunity to get out for a while.

When I arrived at the apartment complex, I found my way to the little community room, which they often allowed tenants to use for small parties. Rose and Charlie Rich were the host and hostess and this was their apartment building. After the drive down from Kokomo, I had to use the bathroom, which was typical for me. I can't go an hour without having to pee! So, I hustled my way to the restroom, not really paying attention to the woman who followed behind me.

While I am in the stall, taking care of the business at hand, I hear this tiny voice say, "Hi, are you Debbie?" Seeing how nothing in my life is completely normal, I just rolled my eyes and said, "Yup, that's me." *Good God, can't a girl pee?* She then says, "Oh, good! I have a message for you and the guy won't leave me alone! He's quite annoying, in fact!" All I could say was, "Umkay, hang on a sec."

When I came out of the stall there, standing nearly directly in front of the door was this kind of strange looking woman. I don't mean that she was unattractive, but she was dressed in this kind of huge, flowery, "Mrs. Roper"-looking caftan with tons of baubles and beads, huge earrings and even bigger bright red hair. She said, "I have a message from your husband." I told her my husband was dead and all she said was, "Yeah, I know." Like it was no big deal.

She said, "He wants you to know that what happened at the cemetery the other day means nothing; that he is always with you." *That* got my attention. The day before the party, I had visited his grave, as I had done almost every day since I buried him there. On the previous visit, I had placed some flowers on his grave. When I returned the next time, the flowers that I had put there were flung all over the graveyard and some strange flowers were now on the grave. I immediately knew who had done it. It hurt my feelings so much that I started to cry as I gathered up my flowers and put them back on his grave. And I sat there for a long time, just crying. I *never* told a *living* soul about this. So, when this woman spoke to me, I listened.

She then proceeded to tell me that my husband had found someone to "take care of me." (I don't know why he always thought I needed to be taken care of and protected, but he did) He was going to be a tall blonde man with a mustache and blue eyes who would use a word that was my husband's word. And this would be my sign that he was the one.

Later that night, I told my friend, Rose, about this. I also told my mom and a friend of my late husband, Bob, who had been helping me with stuff around the house. Then, I forgot it.

Fast-forward to a few months down the road. I was starting to feel lonely. I was not from this town and didn't really know anyone except Bob and his family. I was starting to feel like I wanted to meet some people, make some friends, and maybe find someone just to go see a movie with or have dinner with. I was *never-ever* going to remarry and really didn't want a boyfriend, just a companion. I was still young; only 34. I was starting to regain my footing and was getting back to living again. Bob commented that he knew a guy at work who might be a good friend for me. He said the guy was a diehard bachelor and that I would *never* have to worry about him wanting to get married. In fact, he might even be the king of the "He-man woman hater's club," thanks to a very nasty ex-wife and a divorce. I thought *great*, sounds like a winner.

Bob gave me his email address and I shot him off a quick note introducing myself and basically asking him if he would be my friend! Ha! We exchanged a bunch of emails, (which I *still* have) and, during one of the exchanges, he said something that triggered the memory of that night in the bathroom with that weird lady. He said, "I'd love for you to come by some time with the boys, so they can see my "compukers." He even put the word in quotation marks. "Compukers' was a word that K.O. had always used to describe his homemade computers because they would get him so frustrated, they would make him want to puke.

I called Bob. I had a bunch of questions about Dave. What did he look like? "Well, he's tall, maybe 6'3' or 6'4"?" What color is his hair? "Blonde." Does he have a mustache? "Yeah." What color are his eyes? Then Bob says, "Hell, I don't know, I don't look at guys eyes!" Haha! He said, why are you asking me so many questions about Dave all of a sudden?" I read him the email. When I said the word "compukers" Bob kinda chuckled and said, "I haven't heard that word in a long time." Then he started to say something else but stopped mid-sentence.

I said, "Do you remember what I told you about the crazy lady in the bathroom at that party?" He said, "Yes. I do." Then, all of a sudden, he said, "Oh, hell, no! *Not* Dave! Seriously, K.O.?" Haha!"

I gotta tell you, Dave really had *no idea* what he was getting into with me. After we had officially started dating, I realized that I was going to have to tell him about all the UFO/Paranormal stuff in my life. I was starting to feel guilty, like I was hiding something from him and that it wasn't fair to him not to know. This stuff was such a *big* part of my life, a big part of *me*. I mean, for God's sake, there are books... A lot of the world knows about me and my family thanks to Budd's *Intruders* book and the book I wrote in 1993. I had to tell him, even if it meant losing him. It would be best for everyone if I told him now rather than later. So, I did.

Near the end of one of our dates, I handed him Budd's book, *Intruders,* and the original version of the book you're reading now. I told him I had some things about me that I wanted to share with him and that it was important if our relationship was to go any further. If you could have seen the look on his face as his eyes scanned those book covers. I swear to God I was thinking, "Well there you go. I'm never gonna see this guy again."

A week or more passed and I hadn't heard from Dave. "Dammit," I thought, "I liked this one." Then, out of the blue one night, the phone rang. It was Dave. He told me he'd read both books. "Well..." I said, hesitantly, "what do you think?" He replied, "Well... I think I know you well enough to know you aren't crazy; you're not a liar. So, the only other option is that you've actually had these experiences, and I want to know more!" All I could think was "hot damn!" What a relief!

Fast forward to the night before he proposed to me. He went to K.O.'s gravesite and told K.O. thank you for sending me to him and promised that he would do everything in his power to take care of me the way K.O. would have wanted.

We celebrated our 25th wedding anniversary in April 2020, and it's been an interesting quarter-of-a-century.

FOURTEEN

The Kokomo Boom

~

Wednesday 16 April 2008

Police scanner traffic:

2225L: Howard County (HC) Dispatch: "Attn all Howard County units; 9-1-1 board just lit up with incoming calls; please stand by... Possible shots fired or an explosion." [Several UI HC units] "Explosion shook my car west northwest of station." "Big boom." "Huge." [UI Kokomo PD units] "Possibly fireworks downtown." "Something big exploded."

2226L: HC Dispatch: "We're getting calls from everywhere on a huge explosion."

2230L: HC Dispatch: "Indiana State Police say possible plane down; no location yet."

2231L: FD Dispatch: [all call] "Attn all units [roll call] west of US 31 and 300 North, possible aircraft down."

223530L: "Tipton County is requesting multiple fire departments from Howard County—they have a huge debris cloud or field. FD Dispatch [all call] "Aircraft down, aircraft down; possible aircraft down."

2237L: [All call] "Assist Tipton County, aircraft down, west of US 31 on 300N."

2241L: UI Watch Commander: "Contact the base [Grissom ARB]; see what they had on radar."

2244L: EMS Dispatch: "Go direct (landline) with ##### [Tipton County EMS]—he has new coordinates: 3 miles West of us at [garbled/blocked]...50 or 60 West and 300 North."

2245L: Tipton County Dispatch: "Engine 31, be advised—extend to 5760 West on 300 North."

2246L: UI Watch Commander: "Okay, since that's the only known location of debris, you wanna set up a perimeter back to the nearest crossroads."

2247L: UI Fire Unit 2: "We're on scene."

2250L: Air 10 (to Tipton Co): "Have you contacted FAA or Black Line?"

2251L: UI: "See a fire northwest of us near the Howard/Tipton county line; can advise no further at this time."

2253L: Tipton Co (to Air 10): "Can you do an air search, see if you can locate anything from the air?" Air 10: "Will advise."

2254L: UI Dep Sheriff: "County, I'm going to [frequency change] Ops One." UI County Dispatch: "With all the confusion, I'd appreciate you staying up on the main channel."

2255L: UI Watch Commander: "County, be advised we have multiple county and state officers; we are going to stage and do a search pattern to the north and west of this location" [or north and west of US31 and 300 North].

2257L: UI Dep Sheriff: "Be advised; talked to a gentleman who saw it come through the air; he advised it was NOT a ball of fire; it was breaking apart, whatever it was, and it was about seven miles west of where we were just at." HC Watch Commander: "County, be advised, have all our units obligated to Tipton County switch over to [frequency change] Incident One, and that way we'll take this off main dispatch." HC Dispatch: "Attention all Howard County units assisting Tipton County; switch to Incident One, Incident One. All regular traffic can stay on Sheriff's Dispatch."

2258L: HC Dispatch: "Affirmative; be advised all their planes are accounted for." UI Sheriff's Deputy: "OK, were they training in the area? Several of the residents in the area report they saw planes they thought were from Grissom in the area." HC Dispatch: "Be advised they told me all their planes were accounted for 30 minutes prior to this happening. Their last plane had come in 30 minutes before this had happened."

2259L: UI Sheriff's Deputy: "Be advised, tune in to [TV] Channel 13; my wife just called and said that national media is saying something just happened north of the north Chrysler plant."

2300L: HC Watch Commander: "OK, the news we're getting is that it's gonna be between [Hwys] 28 and 31." Kokomo PD Dispatch: [partly blocked transmission] "… and then lost it at that point in time" UI Kokomo PD Unit: "10-4, Kokomo, I observed that myself." UI Sheriff's Deputy: "From all the witnesses' accounts, it appears to be somewhere South and West of [County Road] 500 North in Tipton county."

2302L: HC Dispatch: "We've been making every attempt to contact the airport with no answer." UI Watch Commander: "Disregard that; contact Carroll County; just had another witness report it's going to be closer to [Hwys] 26 & 29."

2303L: UI Sheriff's Deputy: "I've had two subjects come up and confirm your original theory about the flare incident."

2305L: HC Dispatch: [partly blocked] "… County; they have had no reports of this incident." UI: "Could you TX my cell phone, reference your situation out there? A guy I work with saw something in the sky."

230905L: UI Sheriff's Deputy: "I just got off the TX with Grissom security forces. They said they have no military in the air, and they have not had any military in the air."

230020L: HC Dispatch: "Sir, can you 10-9 [repeat last] your last that was for Howard County?" UI Sheriff's Deputy: "County, it was actually for [unit] 33; I know he's gonna have the helicopter come up in a little bit. Advise him that if he didn't catch my traffic that Grissom just advised me their security forces advised that there's not any military aircraft that's been up or doing anything in that area because they just contacted Ft Wayne as well, just to make sure. UI Sheriff's Deputy: "Loud and clear; loud and clear, thank you." UI Sheriff's Deputy: "Be advised, we're going back north up into Howard County because we've had different witnesses say they heard a plane fly over their houses; we're going up there and see what we can find out." UI Sheriff's Deputy: "Clear. I'm beginning to think we oughta have either Tri-Central or Western activate their football field lights and let that be our jump-off zone for air support."

2312L: UI Sheriff's Deputy: "County, Mr. ##### also said that, after the explosion, he looked out the west windows of his house and he could see fireballs, he said."

2314L: HC Dispatch: "Be advised we just got off the phone with Indiana State Police. They are calling off their portion of it, however I believe there was supposed to be an ISP unit who was meeting you at [Hwys] 28 and 31."

2315L: UI Sheriff's Deputy: [party blocked] "... that this could be a astrological [astronomical] event."

231510L: HC Dispatch: "Indiana State Police was just notifying us of the same thing. They said they spoke to a meteorologist who said there were several meteor showers in the last few days."

2316L: Engine 31: "Do you want us to continue to search or Signal 9, or what do you want us to do?" UI FD Dispatch: "My advice would be to continue search; we've received enough calls that would say something occurred of a spectacular event; we have no idea where; all of our reports are sporadic on where it's coming through."

2317L: UI EMS Unit: "Word is right now that this may be just a meteorite entering the atmosphere, however I don't believe that."

2319L: UI Sheriff's Deputy: "I've just had a witness, law enforcement on top of that, the description of what they're puttin' out could, more than likely be of astrological [astronomical] incident." UI Sheriff's Deputy: "The sound part of it does make a lot of sense, with that explosion."

2323L: UI Watch Commander: "We're pretty confident this is gonna be an astrological [astronomical] event. Just leave two units out to patrol."

2324L: UI FD Unit: "I don't believe we're gonna find anything; if we were, we would have already."

2328L: UI Sheriff's Deputy: "We're at Deffenbaugh [Street} and about 440 West. Uh, they've seen exactly the same thing. What it sounds like is that it was traveling East to West and disintegrated someplace West of us between here and [Hwy] 29." UI Watch Commander: "I've got another unit pulling up with me now; they had the same incident last night north of Logansport in Cass Count... Go ahead and scale back all law enforcement."

2335L: UI FD Unit: [partly blocked] "... stating that their house shook at 200 North and [Hwy] 19, and they're wondering what's going on."

2336L: "We're staging in Curtisville, however we have no debris field, we have no information that anything's burnin' on the ground; Howard County is scaling back, and they will have two officers available if we locate something. State Police is kinda in the same mode; I believe that we should start scaling back, and send fire units home. We may keep one unit in the area in case we get any other reports to be checked out."

2337L: [partly blocked] "... from the air, not from the ground up. It was from the ground down [corrects self] from the air down; also, Cass County had a similar incident in the last 48 hours; believe it came from an aircraft. We're believing at this point it was either a Grissom aircraft that fired a flare, or something meteorological."

2346L: UI Watch Commander: "Advise all non-Tipton county units they can go 10-8 [back in service] back to their counties."

2356L: Tipton Watch Co: "Suspending all operations in reference to this call."

2359L: UI HC FD Dispatch: "Report of fire in a field behind Pleasant Drive at Bradley Rd [SW of Kokomo; north of HC/Tipton Co line].

0002L: "Witnesses report smelling a [metallic] odor from field."

0005L: UI HC FD Unit: "On scene."

[Scanner goes quiet]

~

There have been many times in my life that I have tried my best to just shut off everything UFO-related. I didn't want to talk about it. I didn't want to think about it. I just wanted it all to leave me alone and let me live my life. Let me be "normal." Somehow that never works out for me.

The event in this chapter, now widely known as the Kokomo Boom, happened at a time in my life when I had started focusing more on paranormal research and less on the UFO phenomena. In early March of 2008, I started seeing things in the sky that made me realize that the UFO side of my life was never going away.

I had been visiting my best friend, who lived about 10 minutes from me. We both lived out in the country, south of town. On the way home that evening, just after sunset, in the western sky, I noticed an orange ball of light. It was pretty bright and it caught my eye immediately. Within seconds, another ball of orange light appeared. At this point, I pulled off to the side of the country road I was travelling, put my car in park and started watching these two balls of light. It seemed to me as if they were somewhere over the southwest side of town, near a park where I often walked. They also looked like they were pretty low in the sky. They were definitely nothing celestial. I estimated their altitude to be approx. 2000—3000 feet. I could feel that old familiar panicky feeling in my chest start to rise into my throat. When the third light appeared, I rolled up my car window, jerked the tranny into 'D' and floored that gas pedal. I was freaking out. As I barreled down that dusty country road, lined with freshly turned fields on both sides, I watched these three orange orbs do some kind of mesmerizing weird dance in the sky. They bobbed and dipped and swirled around each other. They acted like *no* conventional aircraft could act—and this was before drones were widely available to the public. There were *no* other aircraft in the area.

By the time I hit State Road 26, all three lights had disappeared. They vanished, instantly, one after the other, as if someone were flipping a switch. By the time I got to my driveway, I was physically shaking. When I hopped out of my car, I found myself actually *ducking* as I ran to the front porch, as if I was trying to hide from something above! I laughed at myself for that later, but at the time it was *not* funny. As soon as I hit the door, I was frantically telling my husband what I had seen and how bizarre it was. His reaction was not as I had expected. He kinda blew it off as if I was just mistaking aircraft for something else. But I *knew* these were no conventional aircraft. My Spidey senses were spinning like crazy and they hadn't done that for years. It was then that I decided I was going to prove to him that I saw these things and they were not normal. I started carrying a video camera in my car.

On April 8, 2008, I posted the following on my blog:

> Something big is going on. I am not sure what it is but it is *big*. I have been pondering it for months, trying to figure out if it is a personal psychic moment. Sometimes I have those psychic moments where I actually can sense something about to happen and then something does happen. Or if this is bigger than me. I believe it is the latter. I have a feeling something *huge* is about to drop out of the sky onto our heads. Something so outrageous that *no one* in the whole world will be able to deny anything anymore. And all hell is going to break loose afterwards. I have been having dreams of me fighting battles like some kind of guerrilla fighter. But I can't see who or what I am fighting.

April 16, 2008 was a hell of a night, and one that drop-kicked me back into the UFO world. I had been spending *all* of my free time watching the skies for these orange balls of light. I had seen them again on a handful of occasions but was never able to capture them on my camcorder. I took to sitting on my car hood in the parking lot of my favorite park, drinking coffee and waiting. I guess I must have looked like the modern-day Roy Neary from *Close Encounters of the Third Kind*, always watching and waiting for something. I gotta say, I was about as obsessed with these orange orbs as Roy was with Devil's Tower.

On this night—April 16, 2008—I had my camcorder out and had driven to Jackson Morrow Park to watch for the orange balls of light. I had seen them again the day before and the weather was such that I thought tonight might be a good night to see them again. I was *determined* to get these bastards on video tape! I got to the park and shut off the lights on my car. The sun had just gone down. I sat there for about twenty minutes before I got bored and called my friend Tim, in Florida. I think we were on the phone for about 10 minutes when the orange ball of light (OBOL) showed up in the north-western sky. It was about 45 degrees from the horizon and it was *really* bright! It was *huge*—like a baby aspirin at arm's length. It was a yellowish amber-orange color, and very sparkly. I reached for the camcorder and the bastard vanished. It quickly grew smaller and then *poof*, it was gone—and there was *nothing* where it had been. No craft. Nothing. There was enough moonlight that I could have seen a big craft, but there was nothing. This is what would sometimes happen, so I got the camcorder up for more.

They would start to pop in, one by one, until two or three or more would appear, and then they would pop out in the same way. Well, this one was the only one. No more came. Something was up. Within a few minutes the sky was absolutely filled with what I called "fireflies." They were small jet aircraft. I could hear them. They were flying in double "V" formations and they were all over the sky where the light had just been. I watched as they made several sweeps of the area. Three or four would break formation and swing back around toward the south and then make a tight turn back to the north. They did not have their red and green wing lights on but they did have on their strobes, so I could follow them, but it made it harder. That "firefly" effect was crazy! They were *everywhere*!

More started showing up and I had a hard time counting them or keeping track of all of them. The sky was crawling with aircraft! *Unbelievable!* After a few minutes they broke away and started moving to the north in small groups. What a show this was! While this was going on, I called a friend of mine—a MUFON investigator in Peru. I had him on the phone telling him what I was seeing. I was really jacked up! I figured he would recognize this behavior as he and his wife are both retired Air Force. He did say that the area I was watching was designated military air space. He lived just north of me so he and his wife went outside and saw some of what I had seen. I had a weird feeling about this spectacle. Like something was wrong. Something was up. Something *big*. For the record, I was sitting in the parking lot at Jackson Morrow, the lot by the volleyball nets. I was facing the west and scanning the sky from north to south. I was just west of US 31 at Center Road (300S).

After the jets left, and it seemed there wasn't going to be any more OBOLs that night, I took my cameras and went home. Besides that, I had to pee. Once I got home (and peed) I stood outside at the end of my driveway for a few minutes, camera in hand, facing west, toward where I had just come from, watching. Waiting for something I could feel in the air. Suddenly, all the animals in the area started howling at the same time. It was the most bizarre thing I had ever heard, so I turned my camera back on and started recording the sound. You can't see anything on the video because it was pitch black outside, but you clearly hear the animals howl and whine. It was at about 10:10pm when I finally gave up and went back inside. I got my jammies on and went into my office to work.

At precisely 10:24pm there was a tremendous explosion outside my window. The window shook, my chair shook, my monitor shook, and it sounded like something fell on my roof and then bounced off. There had been a *huge* flash of light just outside the window in my office that faces southwest. It filled the room with a yellowish light. It all happened so fast I can't recall if I saw the flash before or after the sound. It was damn near simultaneously, I jumped up and ran in to the bedroom and woke Dave up screaming, "Something is wrong, something is wrong!" I still have goosebumps when I think about it! But Dave wouldn't get up! He said he didn't hear anything and fell back to sleep immediately. So, I grabbed a flashlight and ran out in the side yard, in my nightgown, *certain* that I was going to find a parachute or a pilot in my yard, or hanging from my roof. After not finding anything outside, I headed back to my office. Around five minutes later, my son called me. He was a cab driver and at the cab company in town. "Mom, are you guys okay?" he asked. "Yeah, why?" I responded. He proceeded to tell me that a plane has crashed close to our house! I ran back into the bedroom to tell Dave that the explosion was a plane crash. He still didn't wake up. Then, I called the MUFON investigator back. I ran back outside to see if I could smell anything or see anything, like burning embers or the smell of burning fuel. I didn't see or smell anything, but I did hear dogs howling and barking like mad again. I really thought the jets I saw flying all over the place at the park had crashed into each other. And even though I didn't ever find a body or a parachute, I still had images of an ejected pilot in my head.

I went back inside and up to my office to flip on the TV because it was 11pm by now and the news was coming on. First off the bat was a breaking news story—an explosion in Tipton County at the Howard/Tipton County line! They had a caller from Kokomo on the phone. She said that someone reported seeing two bright flashes of light, followed by an explosion. And the report said that there was a *lot* of debris strewn about the area. Then they came back on and said that the FAA in Indianapolis was reporting *no missing* planes! I went to the local police scanner page and pulled up the archives for that time period and, sure enough, there it all was, right there on the audio recordings. I'd hit the jackpot because they hadn't pulled them yet. I downloaded every single one of them. The audio for this event was incredible (and I still have several copies of it).

I believe that the explosion had something to do with the military and with that bright amber-orange light I saw that night. I *saw* that light. I *saw* the jets scramble. I saw it all. I witnessed the bright flash and I felt the explosion that shook my home. I got the howling critters on tape. I just could not believe this. I had been thinking about sky-watching all day. I knew I was going out that night and I had a strong feeling I was going to see something, but I didn't think it would be quite so dramatic! There were a bunch of military jets sweeping that area after the light appeared, and they were flying without their wing lights on. Something was up and I *have no doubt* that the explosion was related to what I witnessed.

The very next morning, I got up early and decided to head out to the area that was considered "ground zero." I knew my way around the back-country roads pretty well, so I grabbed my camcorder and set off on a little investigative adventure.

When I got to the intersection of U.S. 31 and State Road 26, I was in for one huge shock. I had been there only the day before and everything was normal. But now, 26 just west of 31 was not only closed, but *all* of the asphalt was literally *ripped* out. There was *no* way to pass through that road. It was just unbelievable because yesterday the road was normal and this would have had to have been done in the absolute dead of night.

"Hell with you all," I thought, "you aren't stopping me." I had the coordinates for ground zero and I knew how to get there a dozen ways. I backed up and headed south and down through Tipton County. I was excited and nervous at what I might find. As I neared the location of the first report of a "known debris field," I started seeing indications of there having been quite a bit of traffic on the sides of the narrow country roads. You could see where multiple vehicles had been pulled off, some partially into the unploughed fields. Then I started to notice large gouges out into the middle of the fields. They looked fresh. I took lots of photos until a guy on a big-ass tractor just popped up out of nowhere, heading my way. I quickly packed up and got out of there in a hurry. The equipment the man was using looked to be something that turned fields before planting. I didn't stick around to find out what he was doing.

After I saw how the road was just torn all to hell and the condition of the fields, I was convinced that *something* came down there. What, I have no idea to this day. But I have a feeling that someone knows.

In March 2008, around a month before the Boom, a dear friend of mine, who at the time was the State Director for Indiana MUFON, had extended an invitation to me to attend the Spring meeting. I usually didn't attend the meetings because they were typically held in southern Indiana and I live up north. But this time, it was much closer to my home so I decided to go. It would be good to see my friend again and I knew they were going to be talking about the OBAL sightings, which were on the increase in this area. I also wanted to put my two cents in as a witness. It was at this meeting that I met the MUFON investigator in Peru, the one I called that night. Eventually, I was assigned to the Kokomo Boom investigation. No matter how many times I try to shake this phenomenon from my life, it always seems to find me and drags me back in.

In the days following April 16, a whole lot of nonsense began to unfold. I had witnessed this entire event from start to finish, and so I took it personally when I started hearing the lies coming out of Grissom. I was feeling quite pissy about it and decided to write a letter to the editor of the Kokomo Tribune. Eventually the History Channel, The Discovery Channel and UFO Hunters all came out and filmed segments about the Kokomo Boom. I participated in all of these productions. It was an interesting experience. They didn't get it all right, but they got close enough. At least they took it seriously (some more so than others) and they got the information out to the general public. This was a big deal not just to me, but also to Kokomo. To this day, it is still one of this town's biggest mysteries—and I was right smack in the middle of it.

FIFTEEN

And so It Goes

~

Sonmi-451: "If I had remained invisible, the truth would stay hidden."

—David Mitchell

Cloud Atlas

From the circumstances of my conception and birth, to the fact that I have survived multiple life-threatening situations throughout my 62 years, it is clear to me that I am meant to be here and that I am not going anywhere anytime soon. They—whoever "they" are—have made sure that I have overcome whatever life has thrown at me. Mom had told me that she couldn't get pregnant anymore after she had my older sister in 1948. They had tried for years, to no avail. Within months of moving to the house in the neighborhood where the neighbors like to sit on their roofs and watch the UFOs, I was conceived and born. That was in 1959. My mom once said that I was the only kid she had that could fall into a bucket of shit and come out smelling like a rose every time. (She would eventually have two more kids, in quick succession.) I have had not one, but two bouts of Anaphylaxis. Most people die the first time. I developed Eclampsia during the pregnancy with my first son. During the emergency C-section I went into cardiac arrest, coded twice and had a near-death experience during it all. I watched my beloved new husband commit suicide by self-inflicted gunshot. A tornado dropped a house on me, destroyed everything I owned (for

179

the second time in my life), and I basically crawled out from under the debris without a scratch on me. I have been through 2 divorces, widowed once and now currently married to number 4. And this is all what I call "normal" life. I could tell these stories and never once mention anything about UFOs or the paranormal and people would still say, "Aw, hell no."

Sometimes, I wonder if, wherever I existed before this Earthly incarnation, when given the option of what kind of life experiences I wanted to have here, I said, "Hell, with it, just throw them all here; I will just do it all at once so I don't need to come back here again!" That sounds like something I would say. I actually do have very faint memories of having decided to have this experience. It was as if I were in some kind of classroom, looking though a catalog of everything one human could experience. I was like, "Here, I'll take a divorce; wanna see how that will feel. I want to be a mom, too, so throw a baby in there." It was sorta like that. Somewhere in the back of my mind, I felt I had chosen all this before I ever got here.

When I was just kid, I remember having a dream about what I thought was God. I was floating out in space looking at this ball of light in the vast void of nothingness, of darkness. I wasn't afraid but I was curious. Suddenly, this huge ball of light exploded. There was no sound, just this bright blinding flash. When the intensity waned a bit, I could see billions-and-billions of shards of this light that used to be that ball. There were an infinite number of them. They all looked just slightly different in size, shape and color, but they had all come from this ball of light. And something whispered in my ear, "I am." I suddenly realized that this was God. Then, I saw these shards of light enter into people, trees and animals, and everything that was "alive." And suddenly I realized that we were all once part of the same huge ball of light—that we are all one light—and that all of this started with me wondering what was going to happen next. I was just a kid. Clearly, I was different from most kids my age.

I was that kid who lay in her backyard swing-set glider, hair dragging the ground, sneakers up and wrapped around the railing, gazing up at the stars. I wondered who was up there, lying in their own glider, looking up and wondering if *I* was here. I thought about all the things a kid could do in this life—all the things I could imagine—*knowing* this can't be all there is. There *is* more, and I want to experience it. I wished I could talk to them, *again*. I was homesick for a home I had never known, missing people I had never met. Wasn't I supposed to forget? Didn't I already do this once before?

My family life wasn't perfect by any stretch of the imagination. We had our issues, as everyone does. We certainly weren't the Cleavers. But I was definitely not your typical kid, either, right from the start. That is pretty clear now.

For a time in my mid-thirties, I was struggling with all the changes I was experiencing. They were coming fast and hard. Some days I almost couldn't keep up. I started seeing the world and the people I lived with in a whole different light. Sometimes, I felt like I was the only one awake in a room full of sleepwalkers. Recently, I have felt that way again.

Looking back, rereading the words I wrote thirty years ago, I realize I understand more clearly now the things that were conveyed to me. I see the world in a much brighter light, and I realize that most of us can see but a sliver of the wider world around us. In my mind, I envision human beings as tube-type radios in a Dolby digital surround-sound world. Humans are not built to receive or even conceive of all that exists. Just like a transistor radio can't fully receive a television broadcast signal. You might hear the audio but you cannot see the rest of the transmission—the video. We have five (arguably six) senses. And that is how our hardware—our brain—is wired for the world in which we live, for our protection, I believe.

Possibly as a direct result of my early experiences (or by some genetic design bomb before I was conceived) my wiring has been somewhat rerouted. I *think* it is possible that you can rewire yourself with your thoughts and intentions. I believe this was another lesson that something was trying to teach me; I had an epiphany when I heard that EVP I recorded decades ago. When I heard the old man's voice say, "Are the spirits listening?" and the child's voice say, "Can I listen too?" Suddenly, I realized that, in some other dimension, in some other reality, in some other world, *I* was the spirit that someone was listening for. And then I thought of my drawing titled, "Casey's Bubbles" and what I now believe that to signify. I also now feel that at least some of the voices I have captured on digital recording probably aren't spirits or souls that *ever* lived here.

When I drew the picture that I titled "Casey's Bubbles" I felt there was more to the visual than just soap bubbles, but I couldn't put my finger on it. I couldn't verbalize it yet. Now, thirty years later, when I look at that drawing, I see universes. And that smooth flat spot where the soap bubbles touch and become one for a moment, right before the bubble bursts—those are the places where we can have contact with our neighbors in the next universe.

The Electronic Voice Phenomena I've captured since then have mostly been what I call Class A EVPs. They are very clear and there is no mistaking what they are saying. I am an antenna for them, it would seem. My friend Forest Crawford once told me that I was like a bright blue bug zapper in the night sky. I could be seen in the dark from a great distance and attracted all kinds of stuff. I feel like some of these voices are almost like Ham Radio "skip" and "bleed through," where channels that are close together sometimes cross over into each other, depending on atmospheric conditions and disturbances in the earth's electromagnetic field.

I actually have a photograph of an orb that, when blown up, looks for the world like a young face looking up into one of those security mirrors. I also believe there are other "people," for lack of a better term, in these other realities/universes, that are aware of us, who are actively trying to communicate with us, and there are people here working with them. I cannot tell you why I think this is so, but I do. I feel like at least a few of my encounters with strangeness over the years have been of this nature and not extraterrestrial in origin. I fully believe that the reality of our world is far richer and more layered than meets the average eye. Once you have seen it, you can *never* go back to being "asleep."

We are powerful and magnificent beings, capable of *so much* more than we realize. Some people recognize this, but the responsibility that comes with it scares them. And I think there are some who would like for us to remain doubtful of our true potential, because that tiny bit of doubt interferes with the process of self-realization and actualization (*another* thing "they" told me).

I have found that the greater my faith in myself and my abilities, the stronger those abilities become. Our thoughts are powerful and they have a direct impact on the other life forms that we have contact with in our daily lives. Our thoughts have direct impact on our planet and our reality more broadly. I think it's extremely important to pay close attention to your thoughts—conscious and unconscious. They are powerful and can create or destroy. Remember, most of what you see in this world started as someone's thought. Thoughts are just transmissions, like radio waves to the universe. If you want to change something, just think about it in the way that you *want* it to be. Change the message, change the outcome. Simply observing with a different intent can affect the outcome. Once I realized that this was something they wanted me to remember—to know—I was able to change myself from within. I was stronger than I had ever been. My fear morphed into curiosity. The anger became gratitude for having had the experiences. And then *everything* started to change. But it is easier said than done. It requires dedication and consistent practice. Life has a way of distracting me and I still struggle with my negative thoughts and fears sometimes. The world doesn't make it easy. I notice that when I let my negative thoughts get the best of me, shit gets real. Things start to go wrong, I start feeling sick, bad things happen in my world. When I can get control of myself, calm down, let go of my fear and calm my mind, things get better. Negative attracts negative, positive attracts positive. Fear inhibits the actions. I believe "they" were trying to teach me this. And now I get it.

What I'm going to share with you next is going to sound crazy (I mean *really* crazy!). I just want you to know that I am aware of how crazy it is going to sound, and I own it. But I feel it's something important to include here, something that *you* can learn from. At least, that's my hope. Otherwise, I would just keep it to myself.

After we had moved out of the farmhouse and into the house that would eventually be destroyed, I was in the middle of reading a book titled, *E-Squared: Nine Energy Experiments that Prove Your Thoughts Create Your Reality,* by Pam Grout. I had worked my way up to experiment number 4 with some minor success. My problem seemed to be that no matter how much I would try to convince myself I could do it, I still had a tiny bit of doubt. All it takes is that tiny bit, to wreck it all.

We bought the new house at a good price because we knew that we were going to have to replace the roof, the AC unit and the furnace in short order. Everything worked and the roof looked pretty good and didn't leak, but, once we got in, the insurance company insisted that we replace the roof before they would insure it. I was pissed that we were getting this extra stress added to an already stressful situation. Money was already tight from the move. It was costing more than I had planned for and I was having serious anxiety about being about to make the bill and to now come up with a ton of extra cash for a roof I thought I'd have more time to save for.

I was lying in bed one night, unable to sleep. I had been reading my book and I'd done one of the exercises earlier that night. I started thinking about how *great* it would be if I could actually manifest a new roof, a new furnace and a new AC unit. *If* I could just manage those three things, my life would get a whole lot easier and I would feel so much better. As I lay there, I started imagining how I would feel if I got all those things replaced and my finances were stabilized. I nearly dozed off, thinking—no, actually, *feeling*—as if it had already happened, and it felt *so* good. Then, the thought popped into my head to get up and do another session from my book. What could it hurt? I was already awake and maybe I would sleep better if I thought I did some good. So, I got up, went into my office, got the book out and started reading the next lesson. I lit some incense, put on my meditation music and tried to quiet my mind and tune in before I started. Then, I did it. I stood up in the middle of my office, looked up to the ceiling and said, out loud, "Universe, bring me a new roof, a new AC unit and a new furnace. And make it snappy!" Once I was done, I felt drained. I was *really* into it, *really* feeling that it was already happening. I went to bed and fell right to sleep. The next morning when I woke up, nothing seemed different.

Thirty-six hours later, the tornado hit my house. The high end of an F2, its winds were estimated at around 160 mph. We rode it out in the closet and survived. But the roof, the AC unit and the furnace did not. In the end, I got the new roof, the new furnace and the new AC unit, and I learned a very important lesson: when you ask for something from the universe, you gotta be *very* specific about the delivery method! The universe takes the path of least resistance unless specifically directed otherwise. No better way to remove and replace all these things in a hurry than to just blow them all away.

⁓

There you have it. I'm quite certain that I've forgotten to tell you something. I've looked at these chapters at least two-dozen times over the past year. Reading and rereading, then remembering something else I forget to tell you. I am afraid that if I don't end this book pretty soon, I am going to croak before I get it out. Finishing a manuscript and sending it off to the publisher is sort of like saying goodbye to an old friend. There really is no comfortable way to do it and, as soon as they leave, you miss them and want to tell them one more thing. It's a straight up fact that I will be having more epiphanies and experiences, and remembering more as I get older and closer to making that jump to wherever next I land.

If even one sentence in this book has helped you—lifted or reassured you in some small way—then I did what I set out to do. If so, let me know. From the bottom of my heart, thank you for taking the time out of your experience on Earth to read my book and to know my story. For all your support, I am forever grateful.

AFTERWORD

Peter Robbins

~

"Reality is that which, when you stop believing in it, doesn't go away."

—Philip K. Dick

Reading the manuscript for *Extraordinary Contact: Life Beyond Intruders* brought back strong and clear memories of my first meeting Debra Jordan-Kauble and of the two people in our lives without whom we would have never met. More, it reconnected me with the circumstances by which I gained a far deeper appreciation, understanding and respect for UFO abductees and experiencers like Deb and the lives they lead. I am not an experiencer or a UFO abductee, but my sister Helen was, and it was her first telling me about her all-too-conscious memories of being taken at the age of twelve that instantly set me on the path my life has proceeded on ever since.

I was born in Queens New York and lived there until I was almost seven years old. At that time my parents took a deep breath, put a down payment on a modest stucco home built in the 1920s, and moved the family to a village about thirty miles east of the city. Sister Anne arrived on the scene about two years later. Rockville Centre was a wonderful place to grow up, a fact that has only been reinforced over the years in comparing notes with others who had far more challenging childhoods. In that far more innocent time, I was given perhaps the greatest gift any parent can give a child: a happy childhood. Sure. Grandpa died when I was nine. Our cocker spaniel died when I was eleven. And as my hormones began to kick in, I desperately longed for contact with girls completely unavailable to me.

The things I did have going for me though were, upon reflection, priceless. We lived a block from a state park that on non-school days, I was allowed to disappear into for hours on end. This on my bicycle, armed with my cub scout knife, canteen, a sandwich and my imagination. I loved our public library and took pride in borrowing books on any number of subjects. I had a little gasoline powered model plane that I flew in the schoolyard on weekends and trick-or-treated with my sisters and the other kids in the neighborhood on Halloween. I paid close attention to the world of insects in our garden and to the small animals who lived in the park. Compensating for my dyslexia (an as-yet undiagnosed condition that for me manifested in being perennially bad in math), I concentrated on developing my natural talents in drawing and painting. My eyes were already set on becoming one of those people the grownup world called 'artists' when I became a grownup myself.

One subject that literally never crossed my mind though was flying saucers. The exception being the saucers that appeared in the B-movies my friends and I enjoyed at our local movie theater and on television. My mother's parents, Russian Jewish immigrants who lived in Queens, were warm and loving and when I'd sleep over, my Nana would tell me stories of her frightening childhood under the Czar. She also introduced me to the world of black culture through her love of jazz. She inspired my love of cooking, something that she was a true maser of. Dad's parents lived in Manhattan, and on our walks through the city, my Grandpa introduced me to a sense of something called history and ways in which my imagination could enrich my life. Grandma took me to all the museums, to the theater, and never failed to express her outspoken opinion of anything, everything and anyone. As the years passed, I found I had an aptitude for singing and joined every singing group offered by my high school. I acted in school plays, started to go out on dates, found a girlfriend during my senior year, departed for university, transferred to NYC's School of Visual Arts, and (happily) failed my Vietnam era Army physical. After graduating, I got a job as a deckhand on a Norwegian freighter and shipped out for Scandinavia. Upon arrival in Sweden, I departed the ship and ended up traveling a good part of the world on my own. A little more than a year later I returned to New York City where I set about making good on my childhood dream.

By 1975 I was an aspiring painter and photographer living and working in a loft in New York City's Chinatown. I taught painting one night a week at my alma mater, but made most of my living as a carpenter. The real estate boom in Manhattan's Soho District had taken off like a rocket in the early seventies with a wave of loft and building renovations and I had a part in many of them. I considered myself a blue collar intellectual and was proud of the life I had created for myself. Then everything changed. Not in appearance, but in a far deeper sense.

One afternoon in February of 1975, seemingly out of nowhere, a long-forgotten childhood memory returned to me and in no uncertain terms. It was of a UFO sighting. Helen and I had been playing together in front of our house when our attention suddenly shifted to five silvery-white metallic disc-shaped objects coming in at a high rate of speed in a precise V-formation that stopped above the house across the street. There they hung without a sound or a flicker of movement for longer than I'm comfortable remembering. They were close enough for us to make out regular detailing around the edge of each which we later agreed could only be interpreted as windows.

Not a word passed between us as we stared at the objects hovering above us. My mind struggled to make sense of what we were seeing and immediately went into what I've come to term a 'checklist reaction,' namely, reeling off to myself the things they were *not*: planes, kites, blimps, dirigibles, helicopters, balloons, birds, strange-shaped clouds, reflections from the ground, airborne flotsam and jetsam, and finally, in desperation, a boy's final attempt to put a name to them, "secret government test planes. Yeah. They must be some kind of secret government test planes." But they clearly had no wings, no tails, were elliptical as dinner plates held at arm's length at an angle, and in no sense related to conventional aircraft. They were... And that's when I experienced the deepest sense of loneliness I have ever had. If they were representative of the one thing that I was doing my best to evade, then everything I thought I knew, everything I had learned and intuited from my parents, teachers, friends, books, and the world at large was now open to question, and that was simply too much for me to take in. With that, I turned on my heels and headed toward the front door of the house as fast as I could; our mother had to know what we were seeing. Within perhaps two seconds though, my world completely changed yet again.

All anxiety immediately dissolved and was replaced by the feeling I was running through molasses. Everything seemed to have gone into ultra-slow motion and I was filled only with a sense of wonder – completely displacing any thought of the impossible scene I was fleeing. I had lost all motor coordination and was ever so slowly going down, completely captivated by the experience. My final three thoughts before everything went blue for a split second, then black, were, a brief meditation on the ant colony emerging from a scoring in the concrete walkway leading to our front door, how beautiful the pale blue flowers on our mother's hydrangea bushes looked (she was a terrific gardener), and what a beautiful morning it was. Then, *bam*. Oblivion. Now, hold that thought for a moment.

What I have just described to you was by far the single most shattering, life-changing, paradigm-shifting moment I have ever experienced. Period. And that experience is a veritable cupcake when compared to dozens (and dozens) of experiences that Deb Jordan-Kauble can reflect back on in her life. The same can be said for countless other experiencers and abductees worldwide.

My way of dealing with this 'cupcake' was to apply the debunker's mantra: 'It can't be; therefore, it isn't, therefore it must be something else.' I refused to talk with Helen about it when she raised the question later that afternoon, and over the weeks to follow, accomplished the seemingly impossible in submerging the memory so deeply into my subconscious that after a while it was as though it had never happened. A little more than fourteen years later the memory returned. I think I know the reasons why, but they're not germane here. Dissolving into shock, then into tears, I felt, if briefly, that I must be going mad. How could any sane person ever forget something like that I asked myself? I had no idea, but calmed myself down, had a cup of tea, and reviewed my options. Only one emerged and I phoned Helen.

Careful not to blurt out what I'd remembered, I told her I needed to know if she shared a particular childhood memory, then began to set the scene. She cut me off mid-sentence, then told me what I had remembered almost word-for-word. The vindication I felt was momentary as she added, 'But there's more and I don't know how you're going to feel about it,' or words to that effect. And that was when she shared her all too conscious memories of what I would now categorize as a classic UFO abduction experience. Helen clearly recalled my disappearing from her peripheral vision as I turned and ran toward the house, just as she observed a blue beam of light emanate from the underside of one of the objects. Even as a child she knew enough to know that you can't see a beam of light in the daylight, but that was what she remembered, and it was me that was caught up in that beam. She then told me she was lifted off her feet and began to fly upward, hair blowing in the breeze as she looked down to see my prone figure growing smaller, the roof of our house, the neighborhood, everything she knew, receding in the distance. Was she frightened? Not at all. She described the same sense of calm and wonderment I just described to you. Looking up, the discs were only increasing in size, this right up until she found herself inside the one that had beamed down the light.

I listened to what she was telling me in an increasing state of shock. The term she used to describe 'them' was the one she'd invented for herself back then: 'little doctors with big heads and big black eyes who 'talked to her in her head.' She told me of the tall one who she sensed was the leader. Helen remembered how they'd walked her through a curved metal hallway, let her sit in a special chair and look out on the stars, then examined her on a metal table and did things to her, then returned her to the front lawn as I was just beginning to stir. She bent down to see my eyelids begin to flicker, intuited that I was alright, carefully stepped past me, and headed up to her bedroom to consider what had just occurred. Even as I silently raged against the slimmest possibility that what she was telling me was true, I knew, as well as one can know such things, that she was telling me the truth as best she remembered it.

People sometimes invoke the phrase, 'my life changed overnight.' Mine changed in about ninety seconds. I went from actively pursuing a career as a painter to someone obsessed with the UFO phenomenon in general and what had happened to my sister in specific. In the mid-seventies the serious study of UFO abductions was in its pre-infancy and completely absent from television news magazines, talk shows and documentaries, this while the term 'grey' had yet to come into existence. I had no idea there was something called 'ufology' nor that there were organizations and groups which regularly addressed the subject. I felt incredibly alone as I began to educate myself about the phenomenon through books, newsstand magazines and newspaper articles, primarily from the tabloids. My obsession was so all-pervasive that at times it frightened me. Enough so that I sought out a therapist who took the subject seriously and who helped me immeasurably in normalizing my relationship with it. Then one day, about a year into my new life, I was stopped in my tracks by a newsstand headline in a weekly called The Village Voice. It read "Sane Man Sees UFO." I bought a copy, took it home, and read it in one sitting. The article was an account of a UFO incident that had occurred the year before in New Jersey. I had no way of knowing it was the writer's first article on UFOs but was surprised and intrigued to learn that he was a painter as well. But this painter could really write.

His name was Budd Hopkins and there was only one in the city phone directory. I cold called him as soon as I finished reading the article. While kind enough to let me rattle on briefly, the first question he asked me was to describe the kind of painting was I doing, Budd was part of the late period Abstract Impressionist generation while I was a product of the minimalist-conceptualist movement, a school he was not a fan of. But he was interested in hearing more about Helen's experience and invited me to come by his studio. Shortly thereafter we sat down for our first conversation and first cup of coffee together.

Our acquaintanceship quickly grew into a friendship, and then a colleagueship and I was soon working as his studio assistant. The following year we gave our very first UFO talks together in the School of Visual Arts auditorium. In 1981 his first book, *Missing Time,* was published and created a seismic shift in the UFO research community. As more and more of his time and attention shifted from painting to the investigation of UFO abductions, my job morphed into that of research and office assistant. Depending on what needed to be done on a given day, I'd respond to the increasing number of letters he was receiving, take calls, did intake interviews with people who felt they'd experienced missing time or had abduction experiences, sat in on regressive hypnosis sessions, and attended the abductee group meetings he was beginning to hold in his home; sister Helen being one of the original members.

In the summer of 1983, a letter arrived at Budd's home accompanied by an assortment of photographs. It was from a woman in Indiana that described a series of events that had occurred in June of that year and had all of the presenting signs of what he had come to consider a truly significant case. I had to agree after reading it for myself. The photo that stuck in my mind was one of what appeared to be a linear burn mark in the family's yard. After speaking with the woman by phone, Budd decided to visit her and her family. By the time he returned, there was little doubt in his mind that the strange events Debbie and her sister Kathy Jordan had experienced were text-book indications that the Jordan family was caught up in something bigger than they could imagine and that the other intelligences involved were zeroed in on Debbie. Budd was now deeply involved as well. So much so that he had decided to write his second book about her.

That autumn the young woman from Indiana made her first visit to New York City. She stayed with Budd and his wife April and underwent a hypnotic regression. I was unable to get together with them, but it was obvious from what Budd had to say that he thought she was a terrific person. Understandably nervous at times, but extremely courageous despite her fears and possessing a great sense of humor.

Helen and I first met Debbie in the mid-eighties when she attended her first support group meeting at Budd's. She was warmly welcomed into the group and my sister and I were both crazy about her from the get-go. It was especially interesting, and moving, to see Helen and Debbie connect at a break during the meeting. On the surface at least, two more different women would have been hard to imagine. But the two obviously had the makings for a real friendship and were more alike that I think either of them realized. Both warm, smart, caring people linked in sisterhood by events and experiences I could only imagine. Something else happened that night, something wonderful. Deb and I became friends for life and remain in regular contact to this day.

In 1987, *Intruders: The Incredible Visitations at Copley Woods* was published to sensational reviews and very quickly went on to become a bestseller. In 1992 it was made into a CBS miniseries with the brilliant character actress Mare Winningham in the role of Deb. Over the intervening years, Deb Jordan-Kauble has gone on to become an internationally recognized role model for men and women who have been inspired by her courage, straightforwardness, and willingness to make her story public, free of any affect or artificiality. I for one wish her the success she rightly deserves with the publication of *Extraordinary Contact*. And while Budd and Helen are both gone now, I know they would be in complete agreement.

—Peter Robbins
Ithaca, New York,
May 2021

ABOUT THE AUTHOR

~

D ebra Jordan-Kauble is the central figure in Budd Hopkins' classic book, *Intruders: The Incredible Visitations at Copley Woods* (1987), as well as its 1992 TV miniseries adaptation, using the pseudonym "Kathie Davis" to protect her young family. In 1992, she revealed her true identity and co-authored, with her sister Kathy Mitchell, *Abducted! The Story of the Intruders Continues.* Debbie has since made many public appearances and has featured on numerous radio and television shows. For four years, she co-hosted her own Internet radio program, Midwest Paratalk Radio, with Gregg Cable. She has also been an investigator for MUFON and founded her own paranormal research group, the Paranormal Underground. For the last fifteen years Debbie has been employed in the automotive manufacturing industry. She has been an active member of the UAW and the Red Cross. She is a member of MENSA, a licensed cosmetologist, a wife, mother and grandmother. She lives in north central Indiana with her husband, two dogs and cat.

www.ingramcontent.com/pod-product-compliance
Lightning Source LLC
Chambersburg PA
CBHW020154090426
42734CB00008B/821